Library of Shakespearean Biography and Criticism

I. PRIMARY REFERENCE WORKS ON SHAKESPEARE

II. CRITICISM AND INTERPRETATION

A. Textual Treatises, Commentaries
B. Treatment of Specal Subjects
C. Dramatic and Literary Art in Shakespeare

III. SHAKESPEARE AND HIS TIME

A. General Treatises. Biography
B. The Age of Shakespeare
C. Authorship

Series II, Part C

A PICTORIAL HISTORY OF SHAKESPEAREAN PRODUCTION IN ENGLAND

CATALOGUE OF AN EXHIBITION
PRESENTED BY
THE ARTS COUNCIL OF GREAT BRITAIN AND THE
SOCIETY FOR CULTURAL RELATIONS WITH THE U.S.S.R.
1947

A PICTORIAL HISTORY
OF SHAKESPEAREAN PRODUCTION
IN ENGLAND
1576-1946

COLLECTED AND ARRANGED
AND THE CATALOGUE COMPILED
BY
M. ST. CLARE BYRNE

BOOKS FOR LIBRARIES PRESS
FREEPORT, NEW YORK

First Printed: 1947

Second Edition: January, 1948

Third Edition: October, 1948

This edition © M. St. Clare Byrne 1970

Reprinted 1970 by arrangement with M. St. Clare Byrne

STANDARD BOOK NUMBER:
8369-5249-9

LIBRARY OF CONGRESS CATALOG CARD NUMBER:
70-109640

PRINTED IN THE UNITED STATES OF AMERICA

A HISTORY OF
SHAKESPEAREAN PRODUCTION

INTRODUCTION

BESIDE the famous Hogarth engraving of Garrick as Richard III there hangs a Drury Lane playbill (Nos. 11 and 12), advertising Garrick in the name part and Mrs Siddons, as Lady Anne, making her first bid for Shakespearean fame in the London Theatre. This particular specimen is a mid-nineteenth-century forgery. That is why it is there. It looks exactly like the real bill, and it drives home a fact—the fact that not only are we a theatre-loving people, but that already, some hundred or more years ago, we were so keenly interested in our own theatrical history that it was worth while, as a commercial proposition, to forge eighteenth-century playbills. We should probably be the last to give ourselves credit for an interest of this kind. Nevertheless, many who would disclaim all knowledge of the subject, will realise, perhaps with some astonishment, how familiar they are with numbers of these prints. Like Monsieur Jourdain, who was delighted to discover he had been talking prose all his life, they will find that if this is theatrical history they are better acquainted with it than they were aware. These theatrical engravings are as characteristic a product of English popular art as our sporting and topographical prints. We have decorated the walls of our homes with them for nearly a couple of hundred years. They are still there: sometimes handsomely mounted and framed, adorning the gentleman's library, in company with statesmen and divines, scholars and poets, soldiers and great ladies. But more often they have come down in the world: their edges have been sadly trimmed, and they have been pushed into frames too small for them ... trimmed prints, foxed prints, in Hogarth frames with chipped mouldings, in tarnished gilt or heavy black ... with their natural grace and swagger and their inherent drama, outfacing their genteel decay ...

That is how they have always looked. And they have always been there, ranged step by step up the staircase walls, and closely hung along the length of the interminable rambling passages of old-fashioned houses and country inns and hotels. In these surroundings, we take them for granted: are defrauded of our rightful expectation if they have been removed. Here we expect to find Garrick as Lear in the storm scene, cheek by jowl with Landseer dogs and stags: we expect Mrs Siddons to sleep-walk, or, as the Tragic Muse, to rub shoulders with Queen Victoria receiving the news of her accession: here we expect to find Irving as Hamlet and Garrick as Richard III keeping company with Dr Johnson and Henry VIII, and to find Drury Lane alongside of the colleges of Oxford and Cambridge. They are part of the English interior, part of an accustomed background—not museum pieces, but things which we have liked to have about the house for a long time: part of the English interior, but equally, for the present purpose, theatrical history in its liveliest form, and in the one form in which it has made itself genuinely familiar and popular.

Even a small collection like this, concerned only with Shakespeare's plays, presents a visual narrative that unfolds itself clearly and simply and needs little comment to draw attention to the two forces forever at play in the development of the theatre—tradition and experiment. Tradition has given to a few individual characters—notably Falstaff and Richard III—and to a few types such as kings, Greeks, Romans, certain special garments or costumes which appear to derive from the Shakespearean stage. Otherwise, from the Elizabethan period until the early years of the nineteenth century, it gives us 'Shakespeare in modern dress', with a 1768 Macbeth and an 1814 Benedick in smart military uniform, or a Cleopatra, a Hermione, a Juliet and a Desdemona in ravishing Empire gowns. Experiment presents us with John Philip Kemble, in what he believed to be the genuine Roman toga, ousting after two centuries the decorative masque costume *à la romaine* in which his predecessors had portrayed classical characters. And as with costume, so with scenes and acting: their story of tradition and experiment is easily followed. The tradition of eighteenth-century gesture and movement is embodied in the dramatic poses in which the characters are depicted. In the designs for the productions of Kemble, Macready, Phelps and Charles Kean we can follow experiment until it gives us the historical settings which are the new tradition of the eighteen-fifties— the tradition of elaborate spectacle which was to dominate the Shakespearean stage until Granville Barker's challenge in 1912. And then the wheel comes full circle in 1925, when Sir Barry Jackson makes the daring experiment of returning to the older tradition by presenting *Hamlet* in modern dress.

Even the corrupting and the restoration of Shakespeare's text is included in this pictorial history. The extraordinarily spirited *Cymbeline* picture (No. 39), represents a Garrick addition, as does the well-known *Romeo and Juliet* scene (No. 33), which held its own until 1843 and which Hazlitt says 'tells admirably on the stage'. The singing witches of *Macbeth*—originally, with the music, the gift of that early 'improver' Davenant—are to be found in Charles Kean's and Irving's productions; and the interpolated tableau can be found as late as 1899 in Tree's *King John*. Similarly, the restorer can be seen at work in Forbes-

Robertson's *Hamlet*, where Fortinbras appears for the concluding of the tragedy, after having been consistently omitted for over two hundred years.

Eighteenth-century theatrical prints were, in general, the work of artists of distinction, and many of them are finely executed. Whether or not one finds them beautiful is perhaps a matter of taste, but it is a fact that some of the great names in the history of English engraving are associated with these theatrical scenes and portraits, and included in this collection there is work by McArdell, Valentine Green, R. Houston, J. R. Smith, Hogarth, C. Grignion, Pine, G. Dawe, S. W. Reynolds, and S. F. Ravenet.

The nineteenth century provides a more heterogeneous collection of material, and with the Tallis prints (Nos. 65-72) brings into this record the early daguerrotype. Photography proper enters in with the *carte de visite* in the middle years, and one early example is reproduced (and enlarged) here—the photograph of Mr and Mrs Charles Kean in *Macbeth* (see No. VII). Theoretically, photography should make the task of the theatrical historian an easy one for the years after 1890. Actually, the photograph has proved one of the most tantalising, incalculable and perishable of documents, partly because the theatre itself has very seldom been concerned with its systematic preservation. A notable exception is the Shakespeare Memorial Theatre, which acquires the copyright of the photographs it commissions and has available a fine collection of scenic negatives from 1932 onwards. But the theatre in general uses photographs solely for publicity: when the run of the play is over they are no longer needed, and if a management has no permanent abiding in theatre premises the question of storage presents real difficulty. To the newspapers and periodicals the theatrical photograph is inevitably of ephemeral interest, and the material in their reference files is weeded out every few years. There are limits to the stock of negatives which even a photographer can store, and when businesses change hands or disappear old stock tends to disappear also. To these chances against survival we must add losses of complete stocks through enemy action, and the similar destruction of prints, and must also write off the productions which were never photographed *as productions*, and those which were so badly photographed that the record was not thought worth preserving.

Many productions are represented only by studio portraits of individuals, not by photographs of the settings or of groups of players in action. Valuable as these are for the dramatic portraiture of our time, and for the history of theatrical costume, they are not an adequate record of a production. There is also a very natural tendency to concentrate upon small and pictorially effective groupings, to the exclusion óf full-set scenes. More regrettable still, from the historian's point of view, is what the producer calls the 'phoney' photograph—that is, an artificial grouping of the characters in a setting, to give a beautiful picture which conveys the atmosphere and method of the production, but which is not, in fact, a faithful representation of any scene or moment as acted.

Present-day stage photography is capable of such very fine work that a word of warning may be necessary to those who have to base their knowledge of a production like Granville-Barker's *Twelfth Night* (No. 93) solely upon the 1912 photographs. To judge such a production without careful reference to contemporary description, and to take the photographic renderings of colour and pattern as literally as we take these things in the photographs of 1946, would be a grave injustice, as any photographer will explain. The great merit of this pre-1914 stage photography is that it captured the full spectacular effects of the elaborately painted and built-up sets of such productions as Tree's *Macbeth* and *Henry VIII* or Forbes-Robertson's *Hamlet* or Matheson Lang's *Romeo and Juliet*, and has provided us with documentary material of a kind for which we can often seek in vain now-a-days. It is completely in keeping with the English attitude to the theatre that there should be dozens of photographs of the players for any one of the scenes: we have always tended to think first and foremost of the art of the actor and to ignore the art of the production. Now that the balance is being redressed in our dramatic criticism, however, it will be a genuine misfortune for the history of the theatre if the photography of the actual staging should lose anything of the full scope of which it is capable by over-concentration on the close-up.

In a collection of this kind, made for the special purpose of an exhibition, gaps and omissions are inevitable: some of them deliberate, others unavoidable. Limitations of time for the acquisition of material and of space for its display account for some. For example, design, as such, is not represented; but designs have been included when they give the best information we possess to show the appearance of actual scenes, as in the case of Macready's and Charles Kean's productions. In a few instances designs have also been included for the sake of comparison with drawings and photographs of the realised scenes (Nos. 95, X, XIII).

The representation of amateur work has been limited to the universities and schools, on the ground that Shakespearean production is their characteristic if not their only dramatic activity, whereas it is the exception in the programmes of amateur societies in general.

Limitations such as these were deliberate, as was the decision to build up the decade of Old Vic productions as far as possible with photographs which did not duplicate those already available to the student in the

4

Enthoven Collection at the Victoria and Albert Museum. The two really distressing gaps, however, are the complete lack of representation for the early years of the Old Vic (1914-30), and a similar lack for the work of F. R. Benson in the provinces and at Stratford. The first is due to the lack of material. This means, for example, that there is no adequate pictorial record of the 1914 to 1918 seasons, when Dame Sybil Thorndike played all the main women's parts, not to mention the Fool in *King Lear*, Ferdinand in *The Tempest*, and Puck: no record of the 1925-6 season when Dame Edith Evans played all the great rôles; and only a very few items—two of which are included—for the 1929-31 seasons when John Gielgud played fourteen of the outstanding parts, including Romeo and Lear, Richard II and Macbeth, and began his interpretation of Hamlet which, by 1944, was to win from James Agate the tribute, 'This is, and is likely to remain, the best Hamlet of our time'. Fortunately, in the second case, there is no need for Benson's work and the early Stratford days to remain a permanent gap in any future pictorial annals when the material recently presented to the Shakespeare Memorial Theatre by Lady Benson has been arranged and catalogued. It is clear, from the amount available in the Enthoven Collection, that numbers of good photographs exist, though it is to be feared that in most cases the negatives have disappeared.

To 'look into the seeds of time' and speculate upon the probable future of Shakespearean production would be a not-unreasonable exercise for the deductive faculty, after a study of the material which has been gathered for this exhibition. The point to which we have come, however, can be clearly discerned if we consider those photographs which show us the typical modern Shakespearean setting, the self-evident function of which is to achieve as close an approximation as possible to the speed and the methods of an Elizabethan performance. Austerity Shakespeare, dressed in curtains, has fortunately had its day; but it played its part in helping to teach everyone—actors, producers and audiences—the value of speed and the necessity of eliminating waits for scene changing. The decorative value of a set is to-day as highly esteemed as at any time, but its functional quality is a prior charge on the designer's ingenuity; and it is very significant that producers are demanding sets which give them facilities equivalent to those of the Elizabethan theatre—that is, the three acting areas of main, inner, and upper stages. Examples of this may be studied in John Gielgud's *Romeo and Juliet* (No. 98)(2 and 3)), in Michael MacOwan's 1946 *Macbeth* at Stratford (No. XVII,) and in Glen Byam Shaw's *Antony and Cleopatra* (No. 113).

And so, by way of the 1946 *Antony and Cleopatra*, we come back to where we started—to those reconstructions of what, to the best of our

5

knowledge and belief, were the conditions, the demands, the advantages and the drawbacks of the stage for which the plays were originally designed (Nos. 18 and 19). 'In my end is my beginning'. We have re-written Shakespeare, and mangled his texts . . . but he too did some adapting in his time. We have had real rabbits and gold fairies . . . but Shakespeare had a real bear, and his fairies were probably as green as Paul Shelving's. And at last, after three centuries, we have come to terms with his texts in their fulness, without foregoing the natural advantages of our own stage. Tradition and experiment—opposing forces, yet two names for one thing—'the great respirations, ebb and flood, *systole* and *diastole*' that mean a living organism, the living theatre.

M. St Clare Byrne

Plan of the Exhibition

By way of introduction a small preliminary display (Nos. 1-17) presents a synopsis of the story — that is, of the tradition of the theatre until the advent of historical setting and costuming, giving us on the one hand 'Shakespeare in modern dress', and on the other, a few special traditional costumes. The rest of the material is arranged chronologically, save for the final section (Nos. I-XVII) devoted to a single play, *Macbeth,* which presents us with the theme of the whole exhibition in microcosm.

Compiler's Acknowledgments

ACKNOWLEDGMENTS of help and of many kindnesses are on this occasion no mere formality, so that it is appropriate to begin by recording my indebtedness to a friend of long standing, Mrs Gabrielle Enthoven, not only for the practical help given by her and her assistants but for the pleasure and inspiration of a seventeen-years'-old acquaintance with the treasures of the Enthoven Collection, without which I do not imagine I should ever have been tempted into the delightful by-ways of theatrical history.

The exhibition is specially indebted to Mr W. Bridges-Adams for preparing a representative selection of his Shakespearean work at Stratford, as this has had to be largely reconstructed by him from contemporary models and working drawings.

Special thanks are due to the Committee of the Garrick Club for generously permitting the photographic reproduction of three of their pictures and to Sir Kenneth Barnes for sponsoring the request; to Tennent Plays Ltd. and Two Cities Films for gifts of photographs, and to Mrs Frank Gielgud, Mr André van Gyseghem, Mr Osborne Robinson and Mr Richard Southern; to Mr Michael MacOwan and Mr Christopher Hassall for loans; to Mr Walter H. Godfrey for permission to reproduce an original drawing and to the Delegates of the Clarendon Press; to Lenare and to *The Daily Mirror* and to Claude Harris for permission to reproduce copyright photographs of which the negatives had been destroyed; and to Messrs Hutchinson for permission to use in the *Catalogue* á number of illuminating comments from Ellen Terry's *Story of My Life*. I am personally indebted to Mr Tyrone Guthrie, Mr John Burrell, Mr Laurence Irving, Mr John Gielgud, Mr George Rylands, Mr Nevill Coghill, Mr Kyrle Fletcher for help in tracing and obtaining material; to Dame Edith Evans, Dame Sybil Thorndike, Miss Christine Silver and to many friends for information; to Mr W. Blackall, of Cambridge, for the loan of negatives; and not least of all, those photographers who searched for old negatives and gave so ungrudgingly of their time while I looked through hundreds of these in order to find material for the photographic section.

The Exhibition was flown to Moscow and Berlin in 1948. It was exhibited three times in London, at the National Book League, the Whitechapel Art Gallery, and at Leighton House in the Coronation year. On tour it was shown at Shrewsbury, Sheffield, Leeds, Colwyn Bay, Stratford-on-Avon, Middlesborough, Newcastle on Tyne, Guildford, Leicester, Cambridge (Arts Council Gallery), Coventry, Watford, Gillingham, Leyton, Gateshead, Birmingham, Stratford (Lancs.), Preston, Liverpool, Durham, Aldershot.

The Collection is now deposited with the Drama Department of the University of Bristol, where it can be viewed (by arrangement) by students of theatrical history.

CATALOGUE

1. MRS SIDDONS AS THE TRAGIC MUSE: painted by Sir Joshua Reynolds, engraved J. Webb; line and mezzotint: coloured. 1798.

2. RALPH RICHARDSON AS FALSTAFF: Old Vic, *Henry IV* (Pts. 1 and 2). 1945. (*Photograph, John. Vickers*).

3. SPRANGER BARRY AND (?) MRS ELMY IN HAMLET (III iv:) painting by Francis Hayman (49½ × 40): in the possession of the Garrick Club (No. 115): ? *c.* 1748.

   Barry made his first Drury Lane appearance as Hamlet on 24 March, 1747. Note the traditional ungartered stocking (cf. Nos. 31, 48, etc.): Charles Kean is said to have been the first actor of repute to give up this 'down-gyv'd to ankle' convention. Barry wears a grey wig: the Queen has unpowdered brown hair, and wears a red velvet gown with white underskirt. The painting was originally catalogued by Charles Mathews as *Betterton and the earlie. Mrs Barry*, and is generally referred to under this title. Costumes and hair styles contradict the earlier date, and C. K. Adams in the Garrick Club *Catalogue* calls attention to the evident likeness to Spranger Barry in No. 31. For the traditional overturned chair cf. Nos. 31 and 24. For the ghost in armour cf. the Rowe frontispiece to *Hamlet* in No. 24. This would appear to have been normal stage practice.

4. CHARLES MACKLIN (? 1697-1797) as MACBETH (n.d.): MRS HARTLEY AS HERMIONE, 1780: BENJAMIN WRENCH as BENEDICK, by S. De Wilde, engraved Middlemist, 1814: SARAH SMITH as PORTIA, by Emma Smith, engraved E. Scriven, 1808.

   In 1773 Macklin appeared as Macbeth for the first time and is reputed to have introduced Scottish costume. *The London Chronicle* (23-26 Oct.

1773) pointed out, however, that 'Lady Macbeth's modern robes by no means accorded with the habits of the other personages, and Mr Macklin's flowing curls, like the locks of an Adonis, were unpardonably out of character'. His costume here closely resembles that of No. 37. Wrench was a good comedian, but not of the first rank. He first played Benedick at Drury Lane in 1809-10. Oxberry describes his style as that of a 'blood' rather than a gentleman.

5. (1) PEG WOFFINGTON (? 1714-60) as MRS FORD in *The Merry Wives*: painted by E. Haytley, engraved G. S. Shury, 1875. She wears the characteristic side-panniered gown and long apron of the middle of the century (cf. Gainsborough's 'The Artist, His Wife and Child', *c.* 1750; and 'Robert Andrews and his Wife', *c.* 1755, for the head-dress).

   (2) GARRICK as BENEDICK in *Much Ado*: published Wenman; 1778: line: coloured.
   Benedick was one of his best and most successful parts. Frederick Reynolds (*Life and Times . . . Written by himself*: 1826) gives a pleasing glimpse of his performance. Asked by Harris, the manager of Drury Lane, what he liked best in it, Reynolds, then a mere schoolboy, replied 'Where he challenges Claudio', because 'he made me laugh more heartily than I ever did before, particularly on his exit, when, sticking on his hat, and tossing up his head, he seemed to say as he strutted away, Now, Beatrice, have I not cut a figure?'

6. HARRIET FAUCIT (1789-1857) as CLEOPATRA: Mother of the famous Shakespearean actress Helen Faucit.

7. MADAME VESTRIS (1797-1856) as MRS PAGE: in *The Merry Wives*. By S. Lover, engraved S. W. Reynolds, 1826: at least one copy known in

which she is described as Mrs Ford. This particular undated specimen is engraved after Reynolds but is a very inferior piece of work.

8. ELIZA O'NEILL AS JULIET (1791-1872): afterwards Lady Wrixon Beecher. By G. Dawe, engraved F. C. Lewis: 1816: stipple.

    'Her appearance was loveliness personified; her voice the perfection of melody . . . Inferior to Siddons in grandeur . . . she excelled that great mistress of her art in tenderness and natural pathos'. (J. W. Cole: *Life of Charles Kean*).

9. 'SHAKESPEARE IN MODERN DRESS' IN THE 20TH CENTURY.

    1-6. *Hamlet*: 25 Aug., 1925: Kingsway: Sir Barry Jackson's production, directed by H. K. Ayliff. Hamlet, Colin Keith-Johnson; Claudius, Frank Vosper; Gertrude, Dorothy Massingham; Polonius, Bromley Davenport; Laertes, Robert Holmes; Ophelia, Muriel Hewitt; Horatio, Alan Howland; Ghost, Grosvenor North. (*Photographs by Lenare, reproduced by permission from copies in the Enthoven Collection.*)

    8. *Hamlet*: 11 Oct., 1938: Old Vic: produced by Tyrone Guthrie, settings by Roger Furse: see No. 101(3), for cast.

    7. *Troilus and Cressida*: 21 Sept., 1938: Westminster: produced by Michael MacOwan: costumes and settings by Peter Goffin. An open stage was used, and many scenes played against the cyclorama with some very slight suggestion of place, indicated perhaps by one or two pieces of furniture. The Greeks wore pale blue uniforms and the Trojans khaki drill. Nestor, John Garside; Agamemnon, Arnold Ridley; and Ulysses, Robert Speaight, study a town plan of Troy.

10. PLATES FROM VARIOUS SOURCES: showing the mingling of 'modern dress', 'traditional' costumes, and theatrical invention. Note particularly (3), Ferdinand and

Miranda in *The Tempest* (1777), probably accurate for stage costume. Both are completely contemporary in their modes of hair dressing: Ferdinand wears the breeches of the day, the late 18th century stage version of a doublet (cf. Nos. 4(1), 37, 39), and a surprisingly good ruff. Miranda, with her stage queen's train, is frankly theatrical.
(1) Holman as Romeo (1784) probably shows what was worn on the stage, and continued to be worn for forty to fifty years: (cf. *John Bull* 13/12/33), 'The Drury Lane Romeo . . . in his black puffs and bugles'. Garrick as Lear (10) wears the ermine-bordered jacket that marks a king (cf. other examples in No. 29). Henderson (4 and 7) has the traditional Falstaff boots and jerkin. Bensley as Antony (6) is in the *costume à la romaine* tradition.

11. GARRICK AS RICHARD III: engraved by W. Hogarth and C. Grignion, after the painting by W. Hogarth: 1746: line.

    Probably the most famous of all the English theatrical prints. The scene depicted is Richard's awakening from his dream (V iii) in which eleven ghosts—reduced by Cibber to four—have risen in succession to curse him. As they vanish he starts up calling 'Give me another horse! Bind up my wounds!' It was as Richard III that he had originally taken London by storm on 19 Oct., 1741, at Goodman's Fields Theatre. He played it first at Drury Lane on 11 May, 1742. This 'starting from his dream' was always considered one of his greatest moments.

12. PLAYBILL purporting to advertise Mrs Siddons' appearance as Lady Anne, with Garrick as Richard III. Mid-nineteenth century forgery.

13. GEORGE FREDERICK COOKE (1756-1811) AS RICHARD III: drawn and etched by R. Dighton: coloured etching: 1800.

    The only rival, in certain parts, of Kemble and Kean. Byron considered Cooke the most natural, Kemble the

9

most supernatural and Kean the medium between the two, but thought Mrs Siddons surpassed all three of them. Doran (*Annals of the Stage*) says that Richard and Iago were Cooke's most outstanding parts, and that Kemble gave up playing Richard III after Cooke's first season at Covent Garden in 1800.

14. EDMUND KEAN (1787-1833) AS RICH-ARD III: engraved, and printed in sepia: coloured. (V iii): on the eve of battle he traces the plan of the morrow's fighting. 'His manner of bidding his friends good-night, and his pausing with the point of his sword, drawn slowly backward and forward on the ground, before he retires to his tent, received shouts of applause'. (Hazlitt: 15 Feb., 1814).

15-17. TRADITIONAL FALSTAFF COSTUME (cf. No. 2).

15. (*a*) FRONTISPIECE TO HENRY IV (Pt. 2) in ROWE'S EDITION of SHAKESPEARE, 1709.

Falstaff wears 'Elizabethan' ruff, boots, short cloak and slashed doublet, and Mrs Quickly the peaked hat which was still associated with Elizabethan character parts in the early 19th century (cf. Tallis plates of Curtis (*Shrew*) and Mrs. Fitzwilliam (*Wives*) in No. 71). Hal and Poins, as drawers, wear the dress and wig of the early 18th-century gentleman.

(*b*) EDWARD SHUTER (? 1728-76) in HENRY IV (Pt. 2) by Parkinson; plate to *Bell's Shakespeare*, 1776.

16. JAMES HENRY HACKETT (1800-71) as FALSTAFF: Tallis prints: colour. (See Nos. 65-72).

17. ROBERT WILLIAM ELLISTON (1774-1831) as FALSTAFF: drawn and engraved from life by J. W. Gear (n.d.): lithograph: coloured. In 1826 he played Falstaff twice (11 and 15 May), but failed in the part. 'For a brief period after his first appearance [1796] Elliston was held to have excelled Kemble in truth and inspiration . . . With study and a more heroic countenance he would have been on the same level. As it was, *in general excellence*, he may be said, when in his prime, to have been one of the greatest actors of the day'. (Doran: *Annals of the English Stage*).

SIXTEENTH AND SEVENTEENTH CENTURIES

18. A RECONSTRUCTION OF THE SHAKES-PEAREAN PLAYHOUSE: drawn by Noel Hills, and published by Humphrey Milford, Oxford University Press, London. (*Photograph from coloured lithographic broadside; by the courtesy of the Delegates of the Clarendon Press*).

The measurements of the Globe have been calculated by J. C. Adams (*The Globe Playhouse*, 1942) as follows:
an octagon, 84 ft. wide:
the yard, 58 ft. wide:
the stage, projecting 29 ft. into the yard, with a recess 7 to 8 ft. deep:
width of stage, 24 ft. in front, 43 ft. at its widest point, at rear.
He reckons its total capacity as 2,048 persons, the yard accommodating approximately 600.

19. MODERN RECONSTRUCTIONS OF THE SHAKESPEAREAN STAGE (*l. to r.*)

1. THE FIRST ILLUSTRATION TO 'SHAKESPEARE'. (Collotype facsimile from *The Library*, Vol. V, No. 4, March 1925: from the original drawing in the *Harley Papers* in the possession of the Marquess of Bath at Longleat). This drawing, by Henry Peacham, is dated 1595, and illustrates the passage in *Titus Andronicus* (I.i.104) where Tamora, the captive Queen of the Goths, pleads with her conqueror, the Roman general Titus Andronicus, to spare her sons who are about to be slain. The chief interest of the drawing lies in the costumes, and in the evidence it provides to show that the Elizabethans thought of a Moor (and therefore Othello) as coal-black. Titus, Aaron and the sons wear a reasonable stage version of classical costume, which connects with the *costume à la romaine* of the masques and of the 18th-century stage tradition. Two normally-

clad Elizabethan pikemen complete a picture corresponding closely with what we know of the mixture of classic and contemporary costume then used, so that although we cannot prove Peacham saw the play presented like this, we can reasonably say that he is depicting the general idea of Elizabethan stage practice.

2. Reconstruction of the FORTUNE THEATRE in Golden Lane, Cripplegate, 1601: based on the builder's contract, preserved in *Henslowe Papers* (ed. W. W. Greg); from an original drawing by Walter H. Godfrey.
This theatre was used by Edward Alleyne and the Admiral's Men, the chief rivals of Burbage and the Chamberlain's Men, to whom Shakespeare belonged. It was approximately the same size as the Globe, but rectangular in shape, and probably seated some 300 more persons.

3. HENRY VIII: presented in the Elizabethan manner: Shakespeare Memorial Theatre, Stratford-on-Avon.

4, 7. TWO OF WILLIAM POEL'S PRODUCTIONS on reconstructions of the Shakespearean stage: (7) *Hamlet* (1st Quarto): April 1881: St George's Hall: Hamlet, William Poel; Ofelia, Helen Maude Holt (Lady Tree). (4) *Measure for Measure* (II ii): 11 Nov., 1893: at the Royalty Theatre (*from photographs in the Enthoven Collection: Victoria and Albert Museum*).

5, 8. THE MADDERMARKET THEATRE, NORWICH: a reconstruction: Model of the stage, and the stage as used for a production by Nugent Monck.

6, 9, 10 (*down*). The Shakespearean stage as reconstructed for the Two Cities—Laurence Olivier film of *Henry V*, 1944. (*Stills presented by Two Cities Films*).
6. Leslie Banks as Prologue. 9. An upper stage scene. 10. Scene on the main stage.

20. (*a*) THE GLOBE THEATRE, from a 1612 engraving, with the Rose Theatre in the background. 1810.

(*b*) THE SWAN THEATRE: from the 'Antwerp View', 1614. 1809.
(*c*) THE FORTUNE THEATRE (cf. No. 19, 2): by Shepherd, engraved by Wise, 1811.

EIGHTEENTH CENTURY

21 - 25. FRONTISPIECES TO ROWE'S SHAKESPEARE, 1709.
21. *The Tempest.*
22. *Midsummer Night's Dream and Love's Labour Lost.*
23. *Two Gentlemen; Henry VIII; Richard III; Henry VI* (Pt. 2); *Winter's Tale; Richard II; Henry VI* (Pt. 3); *Cymbeline.*
24. *Twelfth Night; Henry IV* (Pt. I); *Troilus and Cressida; Taming of the Shrew; Hamlet; Measure for Measure; Lear.*
25. *Much Ado; Othello; Merchant of Venice.*
(See also 15*a* and MACBETH II*r*).
These illustrations are of real value for indications of contemporary staging and costume, though it is fairly evident that they are not all of equal use. Some—not reproduced here—are obviously compositions in the classical style, and bear no real relation to the theatre. A few of them, such as the *Hamlet, Macbeth, Henry VIII* and *Henry IV, Pt. 2*, are so thoroughly vouched for by other pictorial and documentary evidence that they may be taken practically at face value, and are helpful in setting a standard by which to estimate the relative worth of others. They are full of detail for the history of stage convention—*e.g.* the train-bearers for kings and queens; stage tents; beds with canopies; the over-turned chair in Hamlet's scene with his mother and the ghost; the appearance of the ghost in armour in the closet scene (cf. No. 3); masque costume more or less *à la romaine*, etc. Some points of especial interest are: (*a*) the mixture of 'authentic' historic costume for well-known personages like Henry VIII and Wolsey with the contemporary dress of the 18th-century nobles and gentlemen who form the court in the background; (*b*) one of Richard III's ghosts 'sinking', suggesting trap-work, which was normal 18th-century practice for

ghosts; (c) the Venetian costumes in the court scene in *The Merchant of Venice*, which, if they relate at all to theatre practice, go back to the Elizabethan stage, not forward to the 18th century; (d) the setting for the *Tempest* shipwreck, corresponding closely with the descriptive stage directions of the 17th-century operatised version by Shadwell; (e) the woodland background and the moon in the *Midsummer Night's Dream*, both authentically theatrical in the late 17th century: compare the setting for the wood near Athens with the pictorial background actually used in Settle's 1692 operatised version of the *Dream* known as *The Fairy Queen*: (Act IV) 'a Great Wood: a long row of trees on each side: a River in the middle: two rows of lesser trees of a different kind just on the side of the River, which meet in the middle and make so many Arches'. In scenic directions it is obviously what would be described as 'a deep Grove'—that is, a scene set within the stage space to run most of the depth available, with side wings and a back shutter and possibly cut-out trees. Also cf. Settle's *World in the Moon*, 1697 (Act IV) 'the Scene a Wood, near Thirty Foot high, the Paintings matching in a circle, all the side Pieces and Back Scene cut thro', to see a farther Prospect of a Wood, continuing to the Extent of the House'.

26. (a) Frontispiece to Kirkman's *The Wits* (1672), a collection of 'drolls' or one-act scenes played during the Commonwealth, when, as it explicitly states, 'the publique theatres were shut up': frequently misdescribed, as here, as 'the interior of the Red Bull playhouse': actually an improvised make-shift stage used 'in Halls and Taverns', or even outdoors, by strolling players for a more or less impromptu entertainment. It will be noticed that Falstaff and Mrs Quickly have been borrowed for a scene called *The Bouncing Knight*.
(b) Interior of the Duke's Theatre: built in 1671. Plate taken from an illustration to Settle's *Empress of Morocco* (1673), showing the typical

early Restoration playhouse, preserving the distinction between inner and outer stage (or platform and recess) of the Elizabethan theatre. The inner stage was used for the scenery: the outer was the main acting area. It took nearly a hundred and fifty years, in England, for the stage proper to withdraw itself wholly to the inner side of the proscenium arch.

27. DAVID GARRICK (1717-79) AS HAMLET: painted by B. Wilson, engraved J. McArdell: mezzotint: 1754.
The famous 'start' on seeing the ghost was one of his most discussed movements, apropos of which Boswell enquired, 'Would not you, sir, start as Mr Garrick does, if you saw a ghost?': to which Dr Johnson replied, 'I hope not. If I did I should frighten the ghost'. According to the detailed description given by G. C. Lichtenberg in 1775, when the ghost rose on his trap Garrick was walking upstage, with his back to the audience. At Horatio's call he 'turns sharply, and at the same moment staggers back two or three paces, with his knees giving way under him ... both his arms, especially the left, are stretched out nearly to their full length, with the hands as high as his head, the right arm more bent and the hand lower and the fingers apart: his mouth is open'. (*Lichtenberg's Visits to England*: translated M. L. Mare and W. H. Quarrell, 1938). Wilson's delineation corresponds very closely, except that the pose and the arm and hand gestures are more moderate and even naturalistic than this and other accounts might lead us to expect.

28. GARRICK IN THE STORM SCENE IN KING LEAR; a copy by R. Houston, engraved by C. Spooner, 1761: from the original by B. Wilson, engraved McArdell: mezzotint.
With Kent and Edgar—not the Fool, as is frequently said. Garrick omitted the Fool throughout his career, following the example of his predecessors.

29, 30. PLATES FROM BELL'S SHAKESPEARE:
1776. These plates provide some of
our most reliable evidence for the
costuming of the Shakespearean
characters in the 18th century.
Numbers of them, it will be noticed,
are drawn *ad vivam*.

The conventional theatrical costuming of kings for the history plays, and
the contemporary costume of, *e.g.*
Iago, Macbeth and Mercutio can be
studied in No. 29. *Costume à la
romaine* for the actors, juxtaposed
with contemporary costume (plus a
few theatrical concessions) for the
actresses, and traditional items such
as the plumes worn for tragedy are
well illustrated in No. 30.

31. SPRANGER BARRY and MRS BARRY
in HAMLET: *c.* 1775: probably
painted by James Roberts (48¾ ×
38¼): in the possession of the Garrick
Club (cf. No. 3 for the position and
gesture of Hamlet, and details such
as the conventional over-turned
chair, the ungartered stocking, etc.).
Note the two miniatures on the floor.
The Queen wears a dark blue dress,
bordered ermine, trimmed gold em-
broidery and tassels: powdered hair
(cf. head-dress with Cleopatra's, No.
30). Hamlet is in black: pale blue
sword-belt, edged white: powdered
hair. The neat turn-down of the
stocking top is almost as well ironed
as Mr Wopsle's, and should be compared with Lichtenberg's description
of Garrick's 'disordered' hose (*op.
cit.*). For 'To be or not to be' Garrick
appeared already feigning madness
'with his thick hair dishevelled, and
a lock hanging over one shoulder;
one of his black stockings has slipped
down so as to show his white socks,
and a loop of his red garter is hanging down beyond the middle of the
calf'.

Mrs Barry, born Anne Street (1734-
1801) *m.* (1) Mr Dancer, (2) Barry,
(3) Mr Crawford. She is said to have
equalled Peg Woffington and Mrs
Cibber in tragedy and to have surpassed them both in comedy.
(For Barry, see MACBETH No. I).

32. PLATES FROM BELL'S SHAKESPEARE,
1785-6. (Bell's British Library).

33. GARRICK AND GEORGE ANNE BELLAMY
(? 1731-88) IN ROMEO AND JULIET:
painted by B. Wilson and engraved
by S. F. Ravenet, 1765: line.

This represents one of Garrick's
additions to the text of Shakespeare
and his most important alteration in
this play. In this version, Juliet
awakes just before Romeo dies. It
was first produced at Drury Lane
in 1748. The 1750 text has the
altered scene and the following is the
passage chosen by the painter:
> Romeo ... ... eyes, look your
> last,
> Arms, take your last embrace; and
> Lips, do you
> The doors of breath seal with a
> righteous kiss—
> Soft—soft—she breathes, and stirs!
> (*Juliet wakes*)
> *Juliet*: Where am I? defend me,
> powers!
> *Romeo*: She speaks, she lives, and
> we shall still be bless'd!
> My kind propitious stars o'er-pay me
> now
> For all my sorrows past—rise, rise,
> my Juliet,
> And from this cave of death, this
> house of horror,
> Quick let me snatch thee to thy
> Romeo's arms,
> There breathe a vital spirit in thy
> lips,
> And call thee back to life and love!
> (*Takes her hand*)

Juliet revives and Romeo carries her
from the tomb—presumably down
to the footlights as they were still
doing when Fanny Kemble played
Juliet in the eighteen twenties and
thirties. Then, as the poison over-
powers him, he explains:
> I thought thee dead; distracted
> at the sight,
> (Fatal speed) drank poison . . .
and after another fourteen lines, dies.

34. HENRY WOODWARD (1714-77) as
PETRUCHIO in *Catherine and Petruchio*,
Garrick's adaptation of *The Taming
of the Shrew*: painted by B. Vander-
gucht (an original in the possession
of the Garrick Club, dated 1775);
engraved by J. R. Smith: 1774:
mezzotint.

In the painting he wears a deep cream-white suit laid with silver and white; hat to match, with white plume; pale greenish blue cloak (cf. Bell Shakespeare plate, No. 38). Garrick's adaptation was made in 1754, and held the stage against its original until nearly the end of the next century, except at the Haymarket and Sadler's Wells where there were revivals of *The Shrew* in 1844 and 1856, the Haymarket one being staged in the Elizabethan manner.

35. MRS PRITCHARD (Hannah Vaughan: 1711-68) as HERMIONE in THE WINTER'S TALE: by R. E. Pine, engraved F. Aliamet: 1765: line.
Mrs. Pritchard, pre-eminent in an age of great acting, appears to have had an almost complete range in both tragedy and comedy. She could charm in Rosalind, Beatrice and Millamant: her Lady Macbeth and her Queen Katharine were unequalled for power and dignity. 'Her distinguishing qualities were natural expression, unembarrassed deportment, propriety of action, and an appropriateness of delivery which was the despair of all her contemporaries, for she took care of her consonants, and was so exact in her articulation, that, however voluble her enunciation, the audience never lost a syllable of it'. (Doran: *Annals*).

36. PLATES FROM BELL'S SHAKESPEARE, 1776.
Perhaps the most interesting is Mrs Lessingham as Ophelia (by V. Roberts, engraved C. Grignion). cf. Lichtenberg's description: 'Ophelia's dress . . . after she has lost her reason, is disordered, as far as propriety allows . . . Her long flaxen hair hung partly down her back and partly over her shoulders; in her left hand she held a bunch of loose straw'. (*op. cit.*) The 'disorder' of Mrs Lessingham's dress is not apparent in this *ad vivam* drawing, but the hair is a masterpiece.

37. WILLIAM SMITH ('Gentleman Smith') 1730-1819: as IACHIMO in CYMBELINE: painted and engraved by W. Lawranson: 1784: mezzotint.

The costume he wears is very similar to Macklin's as Macbeth (No. 4.i), and should be compared with that worn by Palmer in the same part (No. 39). Smith was an Eton and Cambridge man, and created the part of Charles Surface. He was the most perfect gentleman of the stage from the fifties to the eighties.

38. PLATES FROM BELL'S SHAKESPEARE, 1775-6 and BELL'S BRITISH LIBRARY EDITION, 1786.
If these plates are compared it is very noticeable how the actresses contrive to dress in the fashion of the moment. Mrs Barnes as Anne Bullen, for example, in 1786 has abandoned the hoops of yesteryear, and so has Mrs Farren as Richard II's Queen and Mrs Siddons as Princess Katharine. All three have adopted the latest thing in very full fichus, which appeared at the end of the eighties and remained fashionable until about 1795.
King's costume as Touchstone is vouched for by his portrait in the Garrick Club collection, as is Woodward's.

39. JOHN PALMER (1745-98) and SAMUEL REDDISH (1735-85) as IACHIMO and POSTHUMUS in CYMBELINE (Act V, Sc. 3): painted by Thomas Parkinson: signed 'Parkinson pinx 1778': (35 × 27): in the possession of the Garrick Club.
This dramatic moment, chosen by the painter, is no more part of Shakespeare's play than is the Garrick *Romeo and Juliet* scene (No. 33). It comes from Garrick's 1761 version.
(*Enter Posthumus and Iachimo fighting. Iachimo drops his sword*).
Post. Or yield thee, *Roman*, or thou diest!
Iach. Peasant, behold my breast.
Post. No, take thy life, and mend it.
(*Exit Post.*).
Iachimo wears a black and white striped costume, white stockings, and red boots (cf. No. 37). Reddish's costume here vouches for the small print in No. 10 (9).

40 & 41. PLATES from BELL'S BRITISH LIBRARY EDITION, 1786. See No. 38.

42. SCENE from TWELFTH NIGHT: painted by Francis Wheatly, engraved J. R. Smith: 1774: mezzotint.

Viola, Miss Younge; Sir Andrew Aguecheek, Mr Dodd; Sir Toby, Mr Love; Fabian, Mr Waldron.
Dodd as Sir Andrew is one of Charles Lamb's best portraits:
'What an Aguecheek the stage lost in him! . . . In expressing slowness of apprehension this actor surpassed all others. You could see the first dawn of an idea stealing slowly over his countenance, climbing up by little and little, with a painful process, till it cleared up at last to the fulness of a twilight conception — its highest meridian. He seemed to keep back his intellect, as some have had the power to retard their pulsation. The balloon takes less time in filling, than it took to cover the expansion of his broad moony face over all its quarters with expression. A glimmer of understanding would appear in a corner of his eye, and for lack of fuel go out. A part of his forehead would catch a little intelligence, and be a long time in communicating it to the remainder'.   (*Essays of Elia*).

NINETEENTH CENTURY

43. (1) ROYAL COBURG THEATRE: now the OLD VIC: by Schnebbelie, engraved by Stow: 1819.
The opening performance, 11 May, 1818; the play was *Trial by Battle*.

(2) INTERIOR of the REGENCY THEATRE in Tottenham Street (on the site of the present Scala Theatre): by Schnebbelie, engraved by Cook: 1817.
The scene is the murder of Desdemona, Othello's entry. The amount of light which was usual in the auditorium until Irving's time is well illustrated by this print.

44. DRURY LANE THEATRE: 1 Oct., 1842: the wrestling scene in *As You Like It*: by T. H. Shepherd, engraved T. H. Ellis.

It will be noticed that there is still a tremendous forestage, but that the proscenium doors have disappeared.

After various unsuccessful attempts they were finally got rid of at Drury Lane in 1822.

45. JOHN PHILIP KEMBLE (1757-1823) as HAMLET: engraved by Jas. Egan after the painting by Lawrence: 1838: mezzotint: proof. The life-size original is in the Tate Gallery, and a smaller version belongs to the Garrick Club. Kemble's black cloak is lined with scarlet and furred with sable. He wears the Order of the Elephant on a pale blue ribbon.

46. (*a*) CHARLES KEMBLE (1775-1854) as OTHELLO: plate from *Thèatre Anglais à Paris*, No. 602: line: coloured: n:d.
(*b*) EDMUND KEAN as LEONATUS POSTHUMUS in CYMBELINE: engraved by I. R. Cruickshank: etching; coloured: plate to *Mirror of the Stage*, publ. Duncombe, 1823.

47. FANNY KEMBLE (1809-93) as JULIET: publ. Skelt, No. 31: coloured Theatrical Portrait, frequently described as 'Twopence Coloured': perhaps the most delightful specimen of its kind. It was as Juliet she made her first appearance on the stage, at Covent Garden, in 1829. Literally pushed on, trembling and inaudible, she recovered her poise in the balcony scene, gave a beautiful performance, and became Covent Garden's leading lady at the age of twenty. She was the daughter of Charles Kemble and Maria Theresa DeCamp, actress.

48. STEPHEN KEMBLE (1758-1822) as HAMLET: caricature: drawn and engraved by R. Dighton: etching: coloured: 1794.

Brother of John Philip, Charles, and Mrs Siddons. A mediocre actor, but stout enough to play Falstaff without padding. This caricature belongs to the period of his management of the Edinburgh Theatre, and is a good example of 'Hamlet in modern dress'. He has the traditional ungartered stocking, and in the rest of his attire is obviously following the example set by John Philip in London in 1783: 'Mr Kemble played the part in a modern court dress of rich black velvet, with a star on the breast, the garter and pendant ribbon of an order—mourning sword and buckles, with deep ruffles; the hair in powder; which, in the scenes of feigned distraction, flowed dishevelled in front and over the shoulders'. (Boaden). His wig shows quite clearly how and why the curious effect as of an electrified hearthrug surrounds Garrick's back in No. IIe MACBETH.

49. THE KEMBLE FAMILY in HENRY VIII: copy, after the painting by G. Harlow (63×85): 1817: engraved by G. Clint, 1819: mezzotint: third proof: 1828.

John Philip as Wolsey; Charles as Cromwell, pen in hand; behind him, Stephen, as Henry VIII; Mrs Siddons as Queen Katharine. Genest says, 'From this print any person who has not seen Mrs Siddons may form a better idea of her figure, face and manner, than from any description of them'. Professor Bell's notes on her performance vouch for the accuracy of the position in which Harlow has depicted her. It was one of her most famous moments. On the line, 'Lord Cardinal, To you I speak', Campeius rose at 'Lord Cardinal'. 'She turns from him impatiently, then makes a sweet bow of apology, but dignified. Then to Wolsey, turned and looking *from* him, with her hand pointing back to him, in a voice of thunder, 'to *you* I speak'.

50. JOHN PHILIP KEMBLE AS CORIOLANUS: engraved by R. M. Meadows after the painting by Lawrence: stipple: *n.d.*

It was in Coriolanus, probably his finest part, that Kemble took his farewell of the stage on 25 June, 1817. Hazlitt considers he surpassed all his contemporaries in this and other characters dominated by 'some one solitary sentiment or exclusive passion' because 'the distinguishing excellence of his acting may be summed up in one word—intensity'. (*A View of the English Stage*).

51. CHARLES KEMBLE AS CASSIO in OTHELLO: by R. J. Lane: lithograph: coloured: initialled by the artist: *n.d.*

'In his hands secondary parts soon assumed a more than ordinary importance from the finish with which he acted them . . . There was no other Cassio but his while he lived'. (Doran: *Annals*).

52. JOHN PHILIP KEMBLE AS HOTSPUR: engraved by Charles Picart, after the painting by J. Boaden: stipple (publ. Chapple, 1820: plate to *Theatrical Inquisitor*). He wears a purely theatrical costume, which, Odell considers 'ridiculous', but which was very much the thing in its day, and gave the same dashing and romantic appearance that the fashionable pantaloons of the first quarter of the 19th century gave to any elegant young dandy with a good leg. Pantaloons were 'correct', according to Beau Brummell, rather than the older buckskin breeches or the new loose trousers.

53. MRS BUNN (1799-1883) as HERMIONE: by M. W. Sharpe, engraved by R. Cooper: (*c.* 1823): stipple and line.

54. HENRY ERSKINE JOHNSTONE (1777-1845) as HAMLET: painted by Sir Robert K. Porter, engraved by J. Thomson: line and stipple: *n.d.* (? 1817).

55. LYDIA KELLY (b. 1795) as DESDEMONA: by J. Partridge, engraved by J. Carver: 1825: stipple: plate to *Theatrical Inquisitor*.

56. GEORGE FREDERICK COOKE (1756-1811) as IAGO: engraved by J. Ward, after the painting by J. Green (original in the possession of the Garrick Club, No. 4) 1801: mezzotint foundation: coloured. Dunlap (*History of the American Stage*) says Cooke 'set all competition at defiance in his Iago'.

57. EDMUND KEAN as OTHELLO: drawn and engraved from the life by J. W. Gear, lithograph: (*n.d.*). Hazlitt con-

sidered that Kean's delivery of 'Farewell the tranquil mind' (III iii) represented 'the highest and most perfect effort of his art'. His voice 'took the deep intonation of the speaking organ and heaved from the heart sounds that came on the ear like the funeral dirge of years of promised happiness'. (*A View of the English Stage*). J. W. Cole, Charles Kean's biographer, considers that 'Othello was unquestionably [Edmund] Kean's masterpiece'.

58. PLAYBILL: KEAN as OTHELLO: 6 Feb., 1822.

59. EDMUND KEAN as IAGO: 'Twopence Coloured': J. Redington: No. 65: *n.d.*

60. The same, as RICHARD III: by J. J. Halls, engraved by C. Turner: 1814: stipple.

61. The same: as RICHARD III, endeavouring to persuade Buckingham to consent to the murder of the young princes. Engraved by Sartain, after W. Nicholas: (*n.d.*) *c.* 1830.

62. (i) JOHN DURUSET (1796-1843) as OBERON; painted by J. Boaden, engraved by Charles Picart: 1819: stipple: plate to *Theatrical Inquisitor*.
(ii) JOSEPH MUNDEN (1758-1832) as AUTOLYCUS; by S. DeWilde, engraved by W. Bond: 1813: stipple: coloured: plate to *Theatrical Inquisitor*.
(iii) WILLIAM BLANCHARD (1769-1835) as SIR ANDREW AGUECHEEK: by S. DeWilde, engraved by Kennerley: 1815: stipple: plate to *Theatrical Inquisitor*.
'He was a mannerist, always walking the stage with his right arm bent, as if he held it in a sling'. (Doran: *Annals*).

63. WILLIAM HENRY WEST BETTY (Master Betty, 'the Young Roscius', 1791-1874) as HAMLET; engraved by J. Alais: (*n.d.*): stipple. Rare, according to *Harvard Catalogue*.
First appeared in Belfast in 1803, at the age of twelve: took Ireland and

Scotland by storm, and worked his way south to London to appear at Covent Garden on 1 Dec., 1804. London also developed Rosciomania, and the child actor was the rage for a season, before being forgotten. As an adult he never earned more than that most damning of contemporary descriptions, 'a respectable actor'.

64. CHARLES KEAN (1811-68) as HAMLET: by A. E. Chalon, engraved E. Morton: 1838: lithograph: with facsimile autograph.
Son of Edmund Kean. He and Samuel Phelps were the outstanding Shakespearean actors of the middle years of the century. He had none of his father's genius, but his ideas of Shakespearean production dominated the English theatre until 1912 and the advent of Granville-Barker. He was the scholar and archæologist in the mounting of the plays, and his tenure of the Princess's Theatre from 1850 to 1859 signalised the triumph of spectacle, of historic costuming, and the discarding for over eighty years of the tradition of 'Shakespeare in modern dress'. Appropriately, therefore, he makes his first appearance here in the Hamlet tunic which became and remained the new traditional attire for Hamlet until the nineteen twenties. (cf. Irving, Forbes-Robertson, Matheson Lang, Nos. 79 (1): 86 (4): (5): 90).

65 - 72. PLATES FROM TALLIS'S DRAWING-ROOM TABLE BOOK, TALLIS'S DRAMATIC MAGAZINE, AND AN EDITION OF SHAKESPEARE PUBLISHED BY J. TALLIS AND CO.: mostly in line and stipple: from original portraits and daguerrotypes: plain and coloured.

These plates cannot compare with the Bell series for beauty, but as a collection they are the 19th century equivalent, being the most comprehensive document we have for information about the costuming of the plays in the time of Macready, Charles Kean and Phelps, in whose companies most of these actors played. Mrs Warner, Laura Addison and Isabella Glyn were Phelps's leading ladies, in succession from 1844 to 1851. Of MRS WARNER's performance in Phelps's 1845 *Winter's Tale* (cf. No. 75 (4)) *The Times* (18/11/45) wrote: 'The famous scene of the statue is so managed as to produce a most beautiful stage effect. The light is so thrown and the drapery is so arranged that the illusion is all but perfect, the stately figure of Mrs Warner, who looks the statue admirably, contributing in no small degree. The moment the curtain was removed, and Hermione discovered, the applause of the audience broke out with immense force'.

MISS GLYN was a pupil of Charles Kemble, and played in the traditional Kemble style. She had 'a fine commanding figure, powerful voice and distinctly masculine manner', in spite of which her best part was Cleopatra.

JULIA ST GEORGE (d. 1903) played in several of Phelps's seasons at Sadler's Wells—as Ariel in the 1847 *Tempest*, and again in 1849: as Fleance in *Macbeth* in 1847, and as Prince John of Lancaster in *Henry IV* (Pt. i) in 1849. Hazlitt's comment on the *Midsummer Night's Dream* fairies at Covent Garden in 1816 would seem to have been still fair comment in the forties: 'Ye full-grown, well-fed, substantial, real fairies . . . we shall remember you'.

MADAME CELINE CELESTE (1814-82) made her only Shakespearean appearance as Princess Katharine in *Henry V*. She was particularly famous in parts which required miming and in doubled and trebled rôles.

The costumes shown in these plates will repay study. The actresses, as usual, are less 'correct' than the actors, and more given to contemporary 'line' and details. Notice the Richard III traditional costume: the general adoption of the knee-length tunic: Malvolio's purely theatrical cross-gartering.

73. DESIGNS FOR MACREADY'S PRODUCTIONS AT COVENT GARDEN: reproduced in positive photostats from George Scharf's drawings in his *Recollections of the Scenic Effects of Covent Garden Theatre, 1838-9: (1839).* Macready took over the management of Covent Garden in 1837, and during his two seasons there played eleven of the Shakespeare plays and *Katharine and Petruchio.* *Hamlet* and *Othello* were put on in Oct. 1837; *Macbeth* in Nov. 1837: *King Lear* on 25 Jan., 1838: *Coriolanus* in March 1838: *The Tempest* on 13 Oct. 1838: and *Henry V* in June 1839. Scharf's drawings give us some idea of what were at that date the most elaborate Shakespearean productions London had yet seen.

John Bull considered that the production of *Coriolanus* 'stands alone in the annals of the stage' (19/3/38) and describes the scene illustrated here: 'We must not pass over the Senate, held in the temple of Capitoline Jove, with its assembled fathers seated in triple rows on their benches of stone, the lighted altar in the midst, the Consul on his curule chair, backed by the bronze wolf to whom Rome owed her founders, with no other ornament than its simple columns, and the vaulted heavens seen through its open roof'.

Fanny Kemble, who played Desdemona to Macready's Othello in 1848, states in her *Records of Later Life* that he 'lets down the bed curtains before he smothers me'. From this, and Scharf's drawing of the earlier production, it would appear that Macready habitually smothered his Desdemonas behind decorously drawn bed curtains.

74. PRISCILLA HORTON (1818-95) as ARIEL: lithograph, retouched with body colour.

Priscilla Horton played in Macready's Covent Garden season of 1838-9 (see No. 73: vii for Ariel in flight). She was a singing witch in *Macbeth,* Ariel flying on wires in *The Tempest,* and the Fool in *King Lear*— the first Fool to appear in *Lear* on the English stage since Nahum Tate cut the character out altogether in 1681. Macready's nerve nearly failed him, in spite of his desire to restore the genuine text to the stage: 'Mentioning my apprehensions that . . . we should be obliged to omit the part, I described the sort of fragile, hectic, beautiful-faced, half - idiot - looking boy that he should be, and stated my belief that it never could be acted. Bartley observed that a woman should play it. I caught at the idea, and instantly exclaimed: "Miss P. Horton is the very person". I was delighted at the thought'. (*Diary*: 4 Jan., 1838). *John Bull* (4/2/38) described it as 'a pleasing performance, giving evidence of deep feeling'. (See No. 73: *Lear*, Act III).

75. SCENIC DESIGNS FOR KEMBLE, CHARLES KEAN AND PHELPS:

1 & 2. Designs by William Capon for Kemble at Covent Garden, 1809: described as 'a composition from extant specimens of the Gothic in England'. Originals in the Shakespeare Memorial Library, Stratford-on-Avon: inscribed 'Wm. Capon inveniet del pinxit Nov. 5th, 1808'. Capon was a genuine antiquarian, and the pioneer of accurate architectural scenery. His earliest scenes were made for Kemble's 1788 production of *Henry VIII*.

3 & 4. Frederick Fenton's designs for Phelps's *Merchant of Venice* and *Winter's Tale* at Sadler's Wells. From photographs in the collection of Richard Southern, who supplies the following note: 'Frederick Fenton and his brother Charles (who was also an actor and played in many of Phelps's productions) were noted scene painters in the second half of the 19th century at the Strand, Lyceum, Old Vic, Princess's and Sadler's Wells theatres. Godfrey Turner wrote that Fenton produced "some of the most picturesque works of illusory art that ever assisted the imagination of playgoing folk". Charles died in 1877, and Frederick, at the age of 82, in 1898'. 3. Act V. Belmont. 4. Act I. The Palace of Leontes. These should be compared with the corresponding scenes on this panel for Kean's productions, Nos. 6 and 11. Of *The Winter's Tale*, *The Times* (28/11/45) says, 'One does not often see a play got up in such a creditable style'.

Designs for Charles Kean's scenery at the Princess's:

5. Stock set for *Hamlet*: by Jones.

6. Belmont: the Avenue to Portia's Mansion: by T. Grieve: *Merchant of Venice*: 12 June, 1858.

10. Shylock's House: by W. Telbin.

8 & 9. *Midsummer Night's Dream*: 15 Oct., 1856. 8. Palace of Theseus and Dance of the Fairies: by F. Lloyds. 9. Entry of Titania and Oberon: by F. Lloyds.

11 & 14. *Winter's Tale*: 28 Apr.: 1856. 11. The banqueting hall of Leontes' palace (I ii): by T. Grieves: 'Musicians were playing the hymn to Apollo, and slaves supplied wine and garlands. Thirty-six resplendently handsome young girls, representing youths in complete war-like panoply, entered, and performed the evolution of the far-famed Pyrrhic dance. The effect was electrical'. (J. W. Cole: *Life of Charles Kean*: 1859).

14. Bacchic Revels (IV iii): by T. Grieves: 'an extensive pastoral scene . . . rich in the luxuriance of Eastern foliage, with a distant view of Nicaea, the capital of Bithynia' (which Kean substituted for Bohemia because it 'affords an opportunity of representing the costume of the inhabitants of Asia Minor'). The drawing shows 'the boisterous merriment of the Dionysia . . . executed by an overpowering mass of satyrs, men, women and children in wild disguises and with frantic energy. There must have been at least 300 persons engaged in this revel of organised confusion, which worked up to a maddening burst at the end when they all rushed out, presenting a perfect revivification of Comus and his Bacchanalian crew'. (*op. cit.*) The production ran without a break for 102 nights.

12 & 13. Properties for *King Lear*: 17 Apr., 1858.

7. CHARLES KEAN AS LEONTES and ELLEN TERRY AS MAMILIUS (1856); (*from a photograph*). In *The Story of my Life*, Ellen Terry describes this, her first appearance on the London stage: 'I can see myself, as though it were yesterday, in the little red-and-silver dress I wore . . . Besides my

19

clothes, I had a beautiful 'property' to be proud of. This was a go-cart, which had been made in the theatre . . . and was an exact copy of a child's toy as depicted on a Greek vase. It was my duty to drag this little cart about the stage, and on the first night, when Mr Kean as Leontes told me to 'go play', I obeyed his instructions with such vigour that I tripped over the handle and came down on my back!'
(*Nos. 5, 6, 8-14: photographs from the original designs in the Victoria and Albert Museum*).

76 IRVING'S ROMEO AND JULIET: 8 March, 1882: Lyceum.

Romeo, Henry Irving; Juliet, Ellen Terry; Nurse, Mrs Stirling; Mercutio, William Terriss.
Scenes: Juliet's Chamber, by W. Cuthbert; Capulet Tomb by W. Telbin.
(*Photographs from the Enthoven Collection, Victoria and Albert Museum*).
The first of Irving's great Lyceum productions, and according to Ellen Terry the most elaborate, and the first to display his mastery of crowds. Of Mrs Stirling she writes: 'She was the only Nurse that I have ever seen who did not play the part like a female pantaloon. She did not assume any great decrepitude . . . Her parrot scream when she found me dead was horribly real and effective'. Of herself: 'As Juliet I did not *look* right. My little daughter Edy, a born archæologist, said: "Mother, you oughtn't to have a fringe".' Of the tomb scene: 'At rehearsals Henry Irving kept on saying: "I must go *down* to the vault". After a great deal of consideration he had an inspiration. He had the exterior of the vault in one scene, the entrance to it down a flight of steps. Then the scene changed to the interior of the vault, and the steps now led from a height above the stage. At the close of the scene, when the Friar and the crowd came rushing down into the tomb, these steps were thronged with people, each one holding a torch. and the effect was magnificent'.
(*Story of my Life*).

77. HENRY IRVING (1838-1905) AS SHYLOCK (1879) AND KING LEAR (1892).
Ellen Terry describes Irving's Shylock as 'quiet', and 'a heroic saint' in the trial scene.
Gordon Crosse (*Fifty Years of Shakespearean Playgoing*) describes his Lear very effectively.
At his first entry he raised his 'huge scabbarded sword with a wild cry in answer to the shouted greetings of his guards'.
'He brought out the human side of Lear and . . . the pity of his story more fully than any actor I have seen . . . He knelt to deliver the curse . . . One of his very best scenes was that in Act IV in which he entered crowned with flowers, his madness having taken a quieter, more fantastic turn. Here his banter of Gloucester was infinitely pathetic, and so was the madman's cunning with which he eluded Cordelia's emissaries, leading up to what was to me the most heartrending moment in the play, the shambling run of his exit at "you shall get it by running".'

78. ELLEN TERRY (1847-1928):
  1. (a) Beatrice (1882);
     (b) Portia (1879);
     (c) Cordelia (1892).
  2. As Imogen in *Cymbeline* (1896).
  3. As Hermione (1906): fifty years after she had played Mamilius with Charles Kean (see No. 75 (7)).

79. 1. HENRY IRVING AS HAMLET: (1874): 'It was in *courtesy* and *humour* that it differed most widely from other Hamlets . . . This Hamlet was never rude to Polonius . . . Hamlet was by far his greatest triumph, although he would not admit it himself'.
(*Ellen Terry: Story of My Life*).
  2. Caricature, by Arthur Bryan: plate to *Footlight Favourites*, No. 2: lithograph.

80. IRVING'S HENRY VIII: 5 Jan., 1892: Lyceum. (a) Souvenir, published by 'Black and White'.
To realise the documentary value of the Irving Souvenirs comparison can be made with the two photographs

and the design for Act I, Sc. 2, on panels (b) and (c). The settings invite comparison with those used in Tree's 1910 production (No. 89). *Henry VIII* is generally considered to have been the finest of the Lyceum productions as a spectacle. It ran for 203 performances. Ellen Terry notes that the costumes were designed by Seymour Lucas, and that Irving had the silk for his robes as Wolsey specially dyed by the dyers to the Cardinals' College in Rome. 'His pride as Cardinal Wolsey seemed to eat him . . . I played Katharine much better ten years later at Stratford-on-Avon at the Shakespeare Memorial Festival'. (*Story of my Life*).

81. FORBES-ROBERTSON'S ROMEO AND JULIET: 21 Sept., 1895: Lyceum. Scenes by Hawes Craven, Joseph Harker, William Harford and T. E. Ryan.
Romeo, J. Forbes-Robertson; Juliet, Mrs Patrick Campbell.
(*Photographs of the scenes from the Enthoven Collection, Victoria and Albert Museum*).

82. BEERBOHM TREE'S KING JOHN: 20 Sept., 1899: Her Majesty's. Souvenir.

TWENTIETH CENTURY

83. BEERBOHM TREE as Richard II (r), Oscar Asche as Bolingbroke, (c.), Brandon Thomas as John of Gaunt (l): in *Richard II* at Her Majesty's, 10 Sept., 1903.
(*Photographs by Lizzie Caswall Smith*).

84. TREE'S MERRY WIVES OF WINDSOR: 10 June, 1902: Her Majesty's: with Ellen Terry as Mrs Page, Mrs Kendal as Mrs Ford, Zeffie Tilbury as Mrs Quickly, and Beerbohm Tree as Falstaff.

For many years this continued to be one of Tree's recurrent and most popular revivals. Ellen Terry describes her dress, designed for her by her daughter Edith Craig, as 'such a *real* thing—it helped me enormously'. Of the production she says: 'The audience at first used to seem rather amazed! This thwacking rough-and-tumble, Rabelaisian horse-play—

Shakespeare! Impossible! But as the evening went on we used to capture even the most civilised, and force them to return to a simple Elizabethan frame of mind'. (*Story of my Life*).

85. MEASURE FOR MEASURE: 20 March, 1906: Adelphi: 'the play produced by Oscar Asche': scenes by Joseph and Phil Harker.
Angelo, Oscar Asche; Isabella, Lily Brayton; The Duke, Walter Hampden; Claudio (centre of large scene), Harcourt Williams.
The photographs illustrate well the normal practice of London Shakespearean production in the early years of this century, as dominated by the realistic Charles Kean-Irving-Tree tradition.

86. (1) SCENE BY TELBIN for George Alexander's 1898 production of *Much Ado* at the St James's: an elaborate, built scene, characteristic of the period. 'Ornate as modern Shakespearean revivals are, this production in point of *mise en scene* holds the first rank . . . The period of the play is indefinite . . . Perhaps the culminating picture is the Church interior, with its realistic acolytes, its chanting friars, its candles, its crosses, its altar, its music, and its heavy incense-laden atmosphere, vividly recalling the same scene as represented at the Lyceum'. (*Times*: 17/2/98).
Alexander played Benedick, Julia Neilson, Beatrice, and Fred Terry, Don Pedro.
(*Photograph from the collection of Richard Southern*).

(2) & (3) JULIUS CAESAR: Beerbohm Tree at His Majesty's, 22 May, 1911, for the London Shakespeare Festival. The forum scene is practically identical with the setting used on 27 June, 1911, for the Command Gala Performance to celebrate the Coronation of King George V.
(*Daily Mirror photograph*).

(4) & (5) MATHESON LANG'S HAMLET: 13 March, 1909: Lyceum: 'produced under the stage direction of Ernest Carpenter': scenes by E. C. Nicholls.

21

Hamlet, Matheson Lang; the Ghost, Frederick Ross; Claudius, Eric Mayne.
(*Daily Mirror photographs*).
'The ghost was cleverly made to appear on the ramparts from the interior of the castle through an apparently massive stone wall'. (*Times*: 15/3/09).

87. ROMEO AND JULIET: 14 March, 1908: Lyceum: 'produced under the stage direction of Ernest Carpenter': scenes by E. C. Nicholls and E. Grimani.

Romeo, Matheson Lang; Juliet, Norah Kerin; Mercutio, Gordon Bailey; Tybalt, Halliwell Hobbes; Benvolio, Lauderdale Maitland; Friar Laurence, Frederick Ross; Escalus, Herbert Bunston; the Nurse, Blanche Stanley.
One of the best sets of photographs to illustrate in detail a typical elaborate London production of the time. (*Daily Mirror photographs*).
The scene of the discovery of Juliet's supposed death derives from the Irving production which included a 'procession of girls to wake Juliet on her wedding morning'. (*Ellen Terry*).

88. BEERBOHM TREE'S TWELFTH NIGHT: This was another of Tree's revivals which continued popular for many years, from 1901 to 1913, but was not one of the great 'spectacles' like *Macbeth* (No. XII) or *Henry VIII* (No. 89).
Souvenir.

89. TREE'S HENRY VIII: I Sept., 1910: His Majesty's. Scenes by Joseph Harker: furniture, costumes and the Banqueting Hall of Wolsey's Palace, designed by Percy MacQuoid.

Henry VIII, Arthur Bourchier; Queen Katharine, Violet Vanbrugh; Wolsey, H. Beerbohm Tree; Buckingham, Henry Ainley: Anne Boleyn, Laura Cowie; Old Lady, Mrs Charles Calvert.
(*Daily Mirror photographs*).
Considered in its own day the *ne plus ultra* of spectacular Shakespeare. 'Sir Herbert frankly offers the whole play as a pageant, a feast for the eye; and he has done the thing from that

point of view as well as it could be done'. (*Times*: 2/9/10).

90. FORBES-ROBERTSON HAMLET: 22 March, 1913: Drury Lane.
Scenes by Joseph Harker and Hawes Craven.

Originally produced at the Lyceum, 11 Sept., 1897, with new scenery by Hawes Craven. It was played by Forbes-Robertson throughout these intervening years and established him as *the* Hamlet of his time. J. H. Barnes was the Polonius of both these productions. Mrs Patrick Campbell was the original Ophelia: Gertrude Elliott took the part in 1913. Others in the 1913 cast were: Claudius, Walter Ringham; Gertrude, Adeline Bourne; Horatio, S. A. Cookson; Laertes, Alex. Scott-Gatty; Fortinbras, Grendon Bentley; 1st Player, R. Ericson; 2nd Player, Robert Atkins. Forbes-Robertson was the first to break with the tradition of ending the play on 'the rest is silence' and to restore the entry of Fortinbras and his soldiers. Hamlet seated himself on the throne as king, died there (No. (*b*), 6), and was then borne away on the soldiers' shields. (*Daily Mirror photographs*).

91. F. R. BENSON AS RICHARD III: F. R. BENSON AND GENEVIEVE WARD AS CORIOLANUS AND VOLUMNIA (20 April, 1910: *Daily Mirror photograph*).
Lady Benson (*Mainly Players*) says: 'Genevieve Ward always joined us to play Margaret in *Richard III* and Volumnia in *Coriolanus*'.

92. THE WINTER'S TALE: 21 Sept., 1912: Savoy: produced by H. Granville-Barker: 'the decoration of the play by Norman Wilkinson, the costumes designed by Albert Rothenstein'.
'It was bound to come. Here, like it or lump it, is post-impressionist Shakespeare . . . It is very startling and provocative and audacious, and on the whole we like it'.
Nos. 1, 2, 5-7. 'For the Leontes-Hermione section of the play, Mr Norman Wilkinson has provided a simple harmony of white pilasters and dead-gold curtains . . . The stage has three planes or steps, with

two side doors in the foreground through which courtiers and messengers make their entrances and exits . . . The act-drop occasionally descends upon the actors when they are speaking . . . so that they begin a speech in mid-stage and finish it before the curtain. Set speeches they deliver at the very edge of the stage (there are no footlights but searchlamps converging on the stage from the dress-circle) addressing them directly to the audience'.
Nos. 3, 4, 8. 'The Old Shepherd inhabits a model bungalow from the Ideal Home Exhibition with Voysey windows'.
Leontes, Henry Ainley; Hermione, Lillah McCarthy; Paulina, Esme Beringer; Perdita, Cathleen Nesbitt; Florizel, Dennis Neilson Terry; Autolycus, Arthur Whitby; Antigonus, Guy Rathbone; Old Shepherd, H. O. Nicholson; Clown, Leon Quartermaine.
'The costumes are after Beardsley and still more after Bakst: the busbies and caftans and deep-skirted tunics of the courtiers come from the Russian ballet and the *bizarre* smocks and fallals of the merrymakers at the sheep-shearing come from the Chelsea Arts Club Ball'. (*Times*: 23/9/12).

93. TWELFTH NIGHT: '15 Nov., 1912: Savoy: produced by H. Granville-Barker: 'the decoration of the play and the costumes designed by Norman Wilkinson'.
'Mr Granville-Barker serenely continues his task of spring-cleaning Shakespeare and of dusting the stage of some of its close-clinging cobwebs of convention . . . A deepish shade of pink is the predominant colour note . . . freely used in conjunction with black, in the costumes and on the various post-impressionist drop curtains'.
Nos. 2, 4, 7-9. 'The rectangular flight of steps leading from [Olivia's] house is fine and bold, but the canopy on the first stage suggests a pink sugar ornament and the two Noah's Ark-like circular boxhedges are obtrusively stiff and ugly'.
No. 3. 'Against this, one must in all fairness put the exquisite little tapestried interior in which the

knights and Maria sing their catches'.
Nos. 11, 13. 'Though the dazzling white and gold is not so extensively used as in *The Winter's Tale*, it is effectively employed for the exterior walls and gates of Olivia's house in the last scene'. (*Referee*: 17/11/12) (An idea of the effect of the pink-white-gold-black colour scheme is given by the coloured cover of *Play Pictorial*, Vol. XXI, No. 126).
Orsino, Arthur Wontner; Antonio, Herbert Heweton; Sir Toby Belch, Arthur Whitby; Sir Andrew Aguecheek, Leon Quartermaine; Malvolio, Henry Ainley; Fabian, H. O. Nicholson; Feste, C. Hayden Coffin; Olivia, Evelyn Millard; Maria, Leah Bateman Hunter; Viola, Lillah McCarthy; Sebastian, Dennis Neilson-Terry.

94. A MIDSUMMER NIGHT'S DREAM: 6 Feb., 1914: Savoy: produced by H. Granville-Barker: the decoration of the play designed by Norman Wilkinson'.
'The general method, of course, needs no description now. We have again the apron stage, the decorative curtains for a background and only two set scenes'. (*Daily Telegraph*: 7/2/14).
1 & 4. *The Palace of Theseus*: 'a place of massive white columns with black decorations and a background of star-spangled black, yielding to glimpses of a reddish purple'. (*Daily Telegraph*). (1) The performance of 'Pyramus and Thisbe'. (4) The Bergomask Dance: 'it never came out of Bergamo but is right Warwickshire, the acme of the clumsy grotesque, with vigorous kicking in that part of the anatomy meant for kicks'. (*Times*: 7/2/14).
2. *A Wood near Athens*: 'the chief woodland scene has very tall, draped curtains for a background, of greens, blues, violets and purples, changing much in tone according to the lights played upon them. The floor is covered with a kind of very rough green velvety material, swelling to a hillock in the centre, on which are white spots indicating flowers'. (*Westminster Gazette*: 7/2/14). 'Over a grassy knoll is suspended a giant wreath of flowers from which depends a light

gauze canopy in which fireflies and glow-worms flicker'. (*Evening News*: 7/2/14).

3. Oberon, Dennis Neilson Terry; Titania, Christine Silver; Bottom, Nigel Playfair; Puck, Donald Calthrop.

'The fairies . . . are gilded from head to foot; faces, necks and hands included. There are, of course, different tones in the gilding, Titania's dress being quite a copper gold: Puck wears a fantastic costume of vivid scarlet, with a huge fuzzy yellow wig and big red berries in it. These gilded fairies, some of them wearing grotesque masks, had a strange non-human air'. (*Westminster Gazette*). (For colour reproductions see *The Illustrated London News* Supplement, Polychromide Process, 2 pp., 11 April, 1914).

95. HENRY VIII: 23 Dec., 1925: Prince's: produced by Lewis Casson: scenery and costumes designed by Charles Ricketts.

King Henry, Norman V. Norman; Queen Katharine, Sybil Thorndike; Wolsey, Lyall Swete; Buckingham, Arthur Wontner.

(*Photographs by Bertram Park*). Of Sybil Thorndike's performance James Agate writes: 'Anything more noble, more dignified, more womanly, or more truly heroical than this Katharine it would be impossible to conceive; and in the ringing challenge of the trial scene Miss Thorndike may be said to have touched the sublime'. (*The Contemporary Theatre*).

Note the simplicity of the Queen's entry at 'Katharine, Queen of England, come into the Court!' (No. 1) in comparison with the elaborately-staged entry in Tree's production (No. 89).

96. TROILUS AND CRESSIDA: 19 June, 1922: Everyman: produced by Frank Birch: scenes and costumes designed by Alec Penrose.

Originally staged, with the all-male cast shown in these photographs, by the Marlowe Society at Cambridge. Transferred with all the undergraduate amateur actors, except those playing women, for a run in London.

l. to r. Ulysses, Dennis Arundell; Cressida, John Seeley; Nestor, V. C. Clinton Baddeley; Calchas; Pandarus, Denys Robertson; Priam; Diomede and Troilus, George Rylands and Rolf Gardner; Thersites; Troilus; Act I: Achilles, J. R. Ackerley; Battle Scene: Murder of Hector.

(*Photographs by courtesy of Hills and Saunders, Cambridge*).

97. OLD VIC PRODUCTIONS:
(1) Lilian Baylis, C.H., M.A.Oxon. (Hon.): Manager of the Old Vic., and the inspiration behind its work. Edith Evans as Emilia and Ralph Richardson as Iago: 7 March, 1932: typical of the long list of distinguished players who have acted at the Vic since its opening in 1914. The Old Vic has been described as 'the boldest experiment in theatrical history'—being nothing less than the establishment in London, at popular prices, of a permanent home for Shakespearean productions. The work of one decade is illustrated here—1931-41: also the Shakespeare productions of the Old Vic at the New Theatre, 1944-46. (*Early photographs, and many of the later, by J. W. Debenham*).
(2) 1931-33: all productions by Harcourt Williams: scenes and costumes by Owen P. Smyth:
King Lear: 13 April, 1931: John Gielgud as King Lear. (*Daily Mail photograph*).
As You Like It: 31 Oct., 1932: Rosalind, Peggy Ashcroft; Orlando, William Fox; Celia, Valerie Tudor; Duke Senior, Alastair Sim.
Midsummer Night's Dream: 2 Nov., 1931: Oberon, Robert Harris; Puck, Leslie French; Titania, Phyllis Thomas; Bottom, Ralph Richardson.
Julius Caesar: 25 Jan., 1932: Marc Antony, Robert Harris; Octavius Caesar, Richard Ainley.
Hamlet: 25 April, 1932: Hamlet, Robert Speaight; Gertrude, Martita Hunt; Claudius, Alastair Sim.
Hamlet: 18 April, 1932: Hamlet, Robert Harris; Gertrude, Martita Hunt; Claudius, Alastair Sim.

Cymbeline: 10 Oct., 1932: Imogen, Peggy Ashcroft; Iachimo, Malcolm Keen.

Twelfth Night: Mar. and May, 1932: Malvolio, Robert Speaight; Feste, Robert Harris; Viola, Edith Evans.

Romeo and Juliet: 6 March, 1933: Romeo, Marius Goring; Juliet, Peggy Ashcroft; Escalus, George Devine; Benvolio, Charles Hickman; Tybalt, William Fox; Capulet, Roger Livesey; Montague, Cecil Winter.

(3) 1933-36:
Twelfth Night: 18 Sept., 1933: produced by Tyrone Guthrie: setting, Wells Coates: costumes, Elizabeth Marsh Williams.
Viola, Ursula Jeans; Olivia, Lydia Lopokova; Orsino, Basil Gill.
Scene: The arrival of Sebastian.

Henry VIII: 7 Nov., 1933: produced by Tyrone Guthrie. Scenes and costumes designed by Charles Ricketts: lent by Lewis Casson.
Henry VIII, Charles Laughton; Queen Katharine, Flora Robson; Wolsey, Robert Farquharson.

Measure for Measure: 4 Dec., 1933: produced by Tyrone Guthrie: settings, Wells Coates: costumes, John Armstrong.
Duke, Roger Livesey; Provost, Ernest Hare.

Richard II: 15 Oct., 1934: produced by Henry Cass: settings and costumes, David Ffolkes.
Richard II, Maurice Evans; Bolingbroke, Abraham Sofaer; Gaunt, Alfred Sangster; Mowbray, Leo Genn.

Julius Caesar: 22 Oct., 1935: produced by Henry Cass: settings, Bagnall Harris: costumes, Betty Dyson.
Brutus, Leo Genn; Antony, Ion Swinley.

Much Ado About Nothing: 5 Nov., 1934: produced by Henry Cass: settings and costumes, David Ffolkes.

Richard III: 14 Jan., 1936: produced by Henry Cass: settings designed by Eric Newton: costumes, Betty Dyson.
Richard III, William Devlin.

(4) 1936:
The Winter's Tale: 17 March, 1936: produced by Michael MacOwan: settings, Bagnall Harris: costumes, Betty Dyson.
Leontes, William Devlin; Polixenes, Douglas Matthews; Hermione, Vivienne Bennett; Paulina, Dorothy Green; Perdita, Ann Casson; Florizel, Geoffrey Keen.

98. (1) HAMLET: 14 Nov., 1934: New: produced by John Gielgud: scenes and costumes designed by Motley.
Ghost, William Devlin; Hamlet, John Gielgud; Claudius, Frank Vosper; Gertrude, Laura Cowie; Laertes, Glen Byam Shaw; Polonius, George Howe; Ophelia, Jessica Tandy; Horatio, Jack Hawkins.
(*Photographs by Bertram Park*).
(2) & (3) ROMEO AND JULIET: 17 Oct., 1935: New: produced by John Gielgud: scenes and costumes designed by Motley.
The production opened with John Gielgud playing Mercutio and Laurence Olivier as Romeo: half-way through the run they changed parts.
Escalus, Alan Napier; Capulet, Frederick Lloyd; Montague, H. R. Hignett; Tybalt, Geoffrey Toone; Benvolio, Glen Byam Shaw; Friar Laurence, George Howe; the Nurse, Edith Evans; Juliet, Peggy Ashcroft; Lady Capulet, Margaret Fielding; Lady Montague, Barbara Dillon.
(*Photographs by Bertram Park, Howard Coster and J. W. Debenham*).

99 SHAKESPEARE MEMORIAL THEATRE, STRATFORD-ON-AVON:
(1) 1919-34:
Director of Festivals, W. Bridges-Adams: at the Old Theatre, 1919-26: at the converted cinema, 1926-32: at the New Memorial Theatre, 1932-34: approximately 130 revivals staged.
The producer's aim was to combine the spaciousness, intimacy and continuity of action of the Elizabethan stage with as much scenic effect as seemed desirable. As a rule, changes were made by the opening or closing of a pair of traverses. Small truck stages were often used and, in the new theatre, full-size moving stages which could raise or roll an entire scene into view and permitted the

construction of scenes more than twice the width of the proscenium opening, any portion of which could be exhibited, according to the action. All productions and designs by W. Bridges-Adams unless otherwise stated, and reproduced by J. B. Charlesworth from the originals.

1. *Julius Caesar, The Merry Wives of Windsor* and *A Winter's Tale*, 1919. Full sets with high cyclorama.

2. *The Merchant of Venice*, 1920· Columns, traverses, truck stages, cyclorama; continuous action.

3. *Macbeth, Richard III* and *Much Ado About Nothing*, 1923; London seasons 1923 and 1924. Semi-permanent settings; continuous action.

4. *Romeo and Juliet*, 1929, and trans-atlantic tours. Semi-permanent settings; continuous action.

5. *The Taming of the Shrew, Measure for Measure, King Lear*; 1928-31 and trans-atlantic tours. Semi-permanent settings.

6. *Twelfth Night*, 1932. Designed by George Sheringham. Viola, Fabia Drake. Olivia, Dorothy Francis. *Hamlet*, 1933. *Much Ado About Nothing*, 1934. Decorated by Reginald Leefe.

7. *A Midsummer Night's Dream*, 1932. Designed as 'a Jacobean Epithalamium' by Norman Wilkinson from models by W. Bridges-Adams. The Wood Scene was set on rolling stages and moved to any position required. Theseus, Wilfred Walter; Hippolyta, Dorothy Massingham; Lysander, Ernest Hare; Demetrius, Eric Lee; Helena, Fabia Drake; Hermia, Hilda Coxhead; Oberon, Giles Isham; Titania, Dorothy Francis; Puck, Geoffrey Wilkinson; Quince, Randle Ayrton; Bottom, Roy Byford.

8. *Julius Caesar*, 1932. Designed by Aubrey Hammond. *Henry IV*, Part 2, 1932. Moving scenes on rolling stages.

9. *The Tempest*, 1934. Designed by Aubrey Hammond from models by W. Bridges-Adams. Costumes by Rex Whistler. The multiple scene closed over the shipwreck on rolling stages.

10. *Coriolanus*, 1933. Inner proscenium and built sets on rolling stages; sunk forestage.

11. *Members of the Stratford Festival Company*, 1932. Theseus, Wilfred Walter; Hippolyta, Dorothy Massingham; Lysander, Ernest Hare; Demetrius, Eric Lee; Titania, Dorothy Francis; Oberon, Gyles Isham; Puck, Geoffrey Wilkinson (costumes by Norman Wilkinson); Malvolio, Randle Ayrton; Viola, Fabia Drake; Orsino, Eric Maxon; Feste, Bruno Barnabé; Sir Toby Belch, Roy Byford (costumes by George Sheringham); Prince Hal, Gyles Isham; Doll Tearsheet, Dorothy Massingham; Falstaff, Roy Byford.

12. *As You Like It*, 1932. Devised and modelled by W. Bridges-Adams. Decoration by Aubrey Hammond and Victor Hembrow. Rosalind, Fabia Drake; Orlando, Ernest Hare. (*Nos. 6, 7, 11, 12 photographs by Claude Harris*).
Romeo and Juliet, 1933. Designed by Norman Wilkinson.
Love's Labour Lost, 1934. Designed by Aubrey Hammond (one scene throughout).
(*Photographs by John Flower*).

(2) 1934-41
(*down*)

1, 10. *Comedy of Errors*: 1938: scenes, costumes and production by Komisarjevsky.

2. *Merchant of Venice*: 1940: Thea Holme as Portia; Baliol Holloway as Shylock.

3, 4, *Midsummer Night's Dream* (1932, '34, '37, '38): setting designed by Norman Wilkinson.

5. Donald Wolfit as Hamlet: 1936.

6. *Othello*: 1939: produced by Robert Atkins: scenes by Gower Parks. Othello, John Laurie; Desdemona, Joyce Bland; Emilia, Betty Hardy; Iago, Alec Clunes.

7, 8. *Twelfth Night*: 1941.

9. *Richard II*: 1941.

11. *Taming of the Shrew*: 1939: scenes, costumes and production by Komisarjevsky.

12. *Julius Caesar*: 1936: scenes and production by John Wyse. Peter Glenville as Marc Antony.

13. *Julius Caesar*: 1932: scene designed by Aubrey Hammond.

(3) CYMBELINE: 1937: produced by Iden Payne: permanent set designed by Gower Parks.
Imogen, Joyce Bland; The Queen, Clare Harris; Cymbeline, Clement McCallin; Iachimo, Donald Wolfit, Cloten, Baliol Holloway; Leonatus, Godfrey Kenton; Guiderius, Michael Goodliffe; Arviragus, Patrick Crean.
(*Photographs by Ernest Daniels, Stratford-on-Avon*).

100. (a) AS YOU LIKE IT and (b) THE TAMING OF THE SHREW.

(a) 11 Feb., 1937: New: produced by Esmé Church: scenes and costumes designed by Molly McArthur.
Rosalind, Edith Evans; Celia, Marie Ney.

(b) 23 March, 1937: New: produced by Claud Gurney: settings and costumes designed by Doris Zinkeisen.
Katharina, Edith Evans; Petruchio, Leslie Banks.
(*Photographs by Angus McBean*).

101. OLD VIC PRODUCTIONS
(1) 1935-36:
Hamlet: 29 April, 1935: produced by Henry Cass: settings and costumes, David Ffolkes.
Hamlet, Maurice Evans; Gertrude, Dorothy Green; Claudius, Abraham Sofaer; Polonius, Morland Graham; Ophelia, Vivienne Bennett; Laertes, Alec Clunes.
Love's Labour's Lost: 14 Sept., 1936: produced by Tyrone Guthrie: settings and costumes, Molly McArthur.
Princess of France, Rachel Kempson; Rosaline, Margaretta Scott; Maria, Katharine Page; Katharine, Rosamund Greenwood.
As You Like It: 10 Nov., 1936: produced by Esmé Church: settings and costumes, Molly McArthur.
Rosalind, Edith Evans; Celia, Eileen Peel; Orlando, Michael Redgrave.
(*Photographs by J. W. Debenham*).

(2) 1937:
Hamlet: 5 Jan., 1937: produced by Tyrone Guthrie: settings, Martin Battersby: costumes, Osborne Robinson.
Hamlet, Laurence Olivier; Gertrude, Dorothy Dix; Claudius, Francis L. Sullivan; Polonius, George Howe; Ophelia, Cherry Cottrell; Laertes, Michael Redgrave; Horatio, Robert Newton; Player King, Marius Goring; Player Queen, Stuart Burge.
Scenes: The play scene, and Ophelia's burial. The curtains and candelabra were removed, and the monument and some tree-tracery on the background added for the change to the latter.
Twelfth Night: 23 Feb., 1937: produced by Tyrone Guthrie: settings and costumes, Molly McArthur.
Viola, Jessica Tandy; Sir Toby Belch, Laurence Olivier.

(3) 1937-38:
Hamlet: 11 Oct., 1938: produced by Tyrone Guthrie: designed by Roger Furse: in modern dress.
Ghost, Malcolm Keen; Hamlet, Alec Guinness; Gertrude, Veronica Turleigh; Claudius, Andrew Cruikshank; Polonius, O. B. Clarence; Ophelia, Hermione Hannen; Laertes, Anthony Quayle; First Player, Craighall Sherry.
Midsummer Night's Dream: 27 Dec., 1937, and 26 Dec., 1938: produced by Tyrone Guthrie: scenery and costumes, Oliver Messel.
Theseus, Gyles Isham; Hippolyta, Althea Parker; Lysander, Stephen Murray; Demetrius, Anthony Quayle; Hermia, Alexis France; Helena, Agnes Laughlan; Oberon, Robert Helpmann; Titania (1937), Vivien Leigh, and (1938) Dorothy Hyson; Bottom, Ralph Richardson.
(*Photographs by Angus McBean, Gordon Anthony, J. W. Debenham*).

102. RICHARD II: 6 Sept., 1937: Queen's: produced by John Gielgud: scenes and costumes designed by Motley.

Richard II, John Gielgud; John of Gaunt, Leon Quartermaine; Bolingbroke, Michael Redgrave; Aumerle, Alec Guinness; Norfolk, Glen Byam Shaw; Queen, Peggy Ashcroft.
(*Photographs by Houston Rogers and Gordon Anthony*).

103. OLD VIC PRODUCTIONS
(1) 1937-39:
Henry V: 6 April, 1937: produced by

Tyrone Guthrie: scenery and costumes by Motley.
Henry V, Laurence Olivier; Princess Katherine, Jessica Tandy.
Richard III: 2 Nov., 1937: Tyrone Guthrie: scenes and costumes, Osborne Robinson.
Richard III, Emlyn Williams; Lady Anne, Angela Baddeley; Queen Margaret, Jean Cadell.

Set built as triptych raised on three steps: doors when closed showing view of medieval London, when open revealing set interiors. Heraldry and banners freely used for court scenes.

Coriolanus: 19 April, 1938: produced by Lewis Casson: settings and costumes, Bruce Winston.
Coriolanus, Laurence Olivier; Volumnia, Sybil Thorndike.

Othello: 8 Feb., 1938: Tyrone Guthrie: settings and costumes, Roger Furse.
Othello, Ralph Richardson; Desdemona, Curigwen Lewis.

Measure for Measure: 30 Oct., 1937: Tyrone Guthrie: permanent architectural setting designed by Frank Scarlett: costumes, John Armstrong.
Isabella, Marie Ney; The Duke, James Hoyle.

Romeo and Juliet: 1939:
Photograph taken during performance at Streatham.
Romeo, Robert Donat.
(*Photographs by J. W. Debenham and Angus McBean*).

(2) 1940-41:
King Lear: 15 April, 1940: the production by Lewis Casson, based on Granville Barker's *Preface* and his personal advice: the text practically uncut: scenery and costumes of the Renaissance period by Roger Furse.
Lear, John Gielgud; Albany, Harcourt Williams; Kent, Lewis Casson; Gloucester, Nicholas Hannen; Edgar, Robert Harris; Edmund, Jack Hawkins; the Fool, Stephen Haggard; Goneril, Cathleen Nesbitt; Regan, Fay Compton; Cordelia, Jessica Tandy.

King John: 7 July, 1941: New Theatre: produced by Tyrone Guth-

rie and Lewis Casson: scenery and costumes, Frederick Crooke.
John, Ernest Milton; Queen Elinor, Esmé Church; Constance, Sybil Thorndike; Blanche, Renee Asherson; Pandulph, Lewis Casson.
(*Photographs by Angus McBean*).

(3) 1940:
The Tempest: 29 May, 1940: produced by George Devine and Marius Goring: décor, Oliver Messel.
Prospero, John Gielgud; Miranda, Jessica Tandy; Ferdinand, Alec Guinness; Caliban, Jack Hawkins; Ariel, Marius Goring; Alonzo, André Morell; Antonio, Marne Maitland; Sebastian, Andrew Cruickshank; Gonzalo, Lewis Casson.
(*Photographs by Gordon Anthony*).

(4) JOHN GIELGUD as KING LEAR (*portrait by Gordon Anthony*).

104. SHAKESPEARE IN THE REPERTORY THEATRES.
(*down*)
1-4, 10-13. BIRMINGHAM REPERTORY THEATRE.
1-4. *Midsummer Night's Dream*: 23 Dec., 1936: produced by Herbert M. Prentice: designed by Paul Shelving.
10. *Winter's Tale*.
11, 12. *As You Like It*: April, 1944.
13. *King John*: 1945: produced by Peter Brook.

5-8. NORTHAMPTON REPERTORY THEATRE.
5, 6. *Othello*: scenes and costumes by Osborne Robinson.
Desdemona's bed-chamber, permanent basic set; and *A Street in Cyprus*, painted curtain for front scenes.

7, 8. *Romeo and Juliet*: scenes and costumes by Osborne Robinson. *A Street in Verona*, painted curtain; and *A Street in Mantua*, painted cloth.

9. THE PLAYHOUSE, LIVERPOOL.
Midsummer Night's Dream: 1928: produced by William Armstrong; settings by Philip Gough.
(*see also* MACBETH XV (1)).

105. THE MERCHANT OF VENICE: 21 April, 1938: Queen's: produced by John Gielgud and Glen Byam Shaw: scenes and costumes designed by Motley.

Shylock, John Gielgud; Portia, Peggy Ashcroft; Antonio, Leon Quartermaine; Bassanio, Richard Ainley; Gratiano, Glen Byam Shaw; Nerissa, Angela Baddeley; Lorenzo, Alec Guinness; Jessica, Genevieve Jessel; Aragon (and Duke of Venice), George Howe; Morocco, Frederick Lloyd; Lancelot Gobbo, George Devine; Old Gobbo, Morland Graham.
(*Photographs by Houston, Rogers and Gordon Anthony*).

106. SHAKESPEARE MEMORIAL THEATRE, STRATFORD-ON-AVON:
(1) 1936-44
(*across*)
1, 4. *Midsummer Night's Dream*: 1944.
2, 6. *The Tempest*: 1938: produced by Iden Payne; settings by Gower Parks.
3. *Coriolanus*: 1939: produced by Iden Payne.
Volumnia, Dorothy Green; Coriolanus, Alec Clunes; Virgilia, Lesley Brook.
4. *Much Ado*: 1939: produced by Iden Payne; settings, Gower Parks.
7. *Much Ado*: 1936: produced by Iden Payne.
8. *King Lear*: 1936: scenes, costumes and production by Komisarjevsky.
9. *Richard III*: 1939: produced by Iden Payne: settings by Don Finley; costumes by Herbert Norris.
Richard III, John Laurie.
10. *As You Like It*: 1939: produced by Baliol Holloway.
Rosalind, Vivienne Bennett; Orlando, Godfrey Kenton.
(*Photographs by Ernest Daniels, Stratford-on-Avon*).
(2) 1940-46
(*down, 3 columns*)
1, 2, 3. Baliol Holloway; as Henry V, 1943; as Shylock, 1940; as Othello, 1943.
4. Clare Harris as Mistress Overdone, in *Measure for Measure*, 1940.
5. *Twelfth Night*: 1945. Malvolio, David Reed; Maria, Mary Honer; Sir Andrew, Peter Bell; Sir Toby, Robert Atkins.
6, 7. *Cymbeline*: 1946: produced by Nugent Monck.
8. Freda Jackson as Audrey, 1940.
9. Thea Holme as Rosalind, 1940.
10. Clifford Weir as Bottom, 1944.

11. Paul Scofield and Ruth Lodge in *Henry V*, 1946.
12. *Midsummer Night's Dream*: 1944: Titania, Patricia Jessel; Oberon, John Byron.
(*Photographs by Holte, Stratford-on-Avon*).
(3) 1946: (*see also* MACBETH XVII; *and above*, 2).
1 & 3. *Measure for Measure*: produced by Frank McMullan: settings and costumes by Otis Riggs.
2. *Henry V*: produced by Dorothy Green: settings by Reginald Leefe: costumes by Herbert Norris Paul Scofield as Henry V.
4-7. *Love's Labour's Lost*: produced by Peter Brook: settings and costumes by Reginald Leefe.
(*Photographs by Angus McBean*).

107. (1) HAMLET: 13 Oct., 1944: Haymarket: produced by George Rylands: setting by Ruth Keating, costumes by Jeannetta Cochrane, 'the play lit by Hamish Wilson.'
Hamlet, John Gielgud; Ghost, Leon Quartermaine; Claudius, Leslie Banks; Gertrude, Marian Spencer; Ophelia, Peggy Ashcroft; Polonius, Miles Malleson; Horatio, Francis Lister; Player King, Cecil Trouncer; Laertes, Patrick Crean.
(*Photographs by Cecil Beaton, presented by Tennent Plays Ltd.*).
(2) MIDSUMMER NIGHT'S DREAM: 25 Jan., 1945: Haymarket: produced by Nevill Coghill: décor by Hal Burton, 'the play lit by Hamish Wilson'.
Oberon, John Gielgud; Titania, Peggy Ashcroft; Lysander, Patrick Crean; Demetrius, Francis Lister; Hermia, Isabel Dean; Helena, Marian Spencer; Bottom, Leslie Banks; Snout, George Woodbridge; Flute, John Blatchley; Quince, Miles Malleson; Snug, Ernest Hare; Starveling, Francis Drake.
(*Photographs by Cecil Beaton, presented by Tennent Plays Ltd.*).

108. SHAKESPEARE FOR THE ARMY: OTHELLO: produced by Captain Stephen Murray for the Army Topical Theatre Unit, under the command of Captain André van Gyseghem. Opened in Cairo, Oct.

1945: toured Egypt, Palestine and the Lebanon, Feb.-July 1946: played alternate nights with ABCA plays. The spot-lights and black curtains typical of the ABCA fit-up were used for the setting. All players were members of the Forces, and either professional actors or else students who had already trained for the stage.

Othello, Alan Badel, sergeant in the Parachute Regiment, active service in Holland and Germany; Iago, A. van Gyseghem; Desdemona, Christine Russell, formerly Amersham Repertory Company.
(*Photographs by Angus McBean*).

109. (*l. to r.*)
SHAKESPEARE IN SCHOOLS.
1 & 2. *A Midsummer Night's Dream:* 1945.
3 & 4. *Romeo and Juliet:* 1945.
5-8 *King Lear:* 1946.
Presented by the Braintree Shakespeare Players. This company of boy players, all under seventeen and pupils of the Secondary Boys' School, Braintree, Essex, was started during the blitz in 1941, and has staged twelve of the plays and given one hundred and sixty performances. Plays are produced by the Headmaster, Mr A. H. Freeman: all scenery, props, furniture, lighting, etc., designed, made and painted in the school workshops. The company does all its own printing. One hundred and eighty boys have been trained in the company. From their receipts of £2,000 to date, fees have been provided for training two former members at the Royal Academy of Dramatic Art. John Gielgud became their president in 1943.
Other productions: *Richard II, Henry IV, Macbeth, Coriolanus, Tempest, Twelfth Night, Hamlet, Taming of the Shrew* and *Merry Wives*.
(*Photographs by Dennis Hatt*).

110. OLD VIC PRODUCTIONS AT THE NEW THEATRE: 1944-45.
(1) *Richard III*: 13 Sept., 1944: produced by John Burrell: scenery by Morris Kestelman, costumes by Doris Zinkeisen.
Richard III, Laurence Olivier; Queen Margaret, Sybil Thorndike;

Queen Elizabeth, Margaret Leighton; Lady Anne, Joyce Redman; Hastings, Michael Warre; Buckingham, Nicholas Hannen; Clarence, George Relph.
(2) *Henry IV*: Pt. 1, 26 Sept.; Pt. 2, 3 Oct., 1945: produced by John Burrell; scenes by Gower Parks; costumes by Roger Furse.
Henry IV, Nicholas Hannen; Prince Hal, Michael Warre; Hotspur (Pt. 1), Laurence Olivier; Falstaff, Ralph Richardson; Mistress Quickly, Sybil Thorndike; Shallow (Pt. 2), Laurence Olivier.
(*Photographs by John Vickers*).

111. SHAKESPEARE IN THE UNIVERSITIES: OXFORD:
(1) *Romeo and Juliet*: 9-13 Feb., 1932: New Theatre, Oxford: produced by John Gielgud for the O.U.D.S.: settings designed by Molly McArthur: costumes by Motley.
With Edith Evans as the Nurse and Peggy Ashcroft as Juliet. Romeo, Christopher Hassall: Mercutio, George Devine; Tybalt, William Devlin; Friar Laurence (and Chorus), Hugh Hunt.
This was John Gielgud's first production. A London performance was given at the New Theatre for the benefit of the Old Vic-Sadler's Wells Fund.
'Mr Gielgud and his designer have set the play in a triptych of arches, giving three separate stages which can be used separately or in combination. Such small scenes as Friar Laurence's cell are set in a single arch; Juliet's balcony and garden extend across two; the big scenes employ all three. Meanwhile, the whole width of the stage in front of the arches is continuously in use. For speed and flexibility, combined with picturesque effect, I have seen nothing better than this method'.
(W. A. Darlington, in *The Daily Telegraph*).

The first Shakespeare production of the Oxford University Dramatic Society was *Henry IV* (Pt. 1) in 1885. Up to 1910 they had presented fourteen of the plays in twenty-one productions. The O.U.D.S. works with professional producers and designers, and professional actresses for the women's parts.

(*Photographs and original costume design lent by Christopher Hassall*).

(2) O.U.D.S. AND FRIENDS OF O,U.D.S. PRODUCTIONS:

Richard III: 1934: performed in Christ Church quadrangle. Peter Glenville as Richard.

Hamlet: 1934: Jubilee performance: produced by Nevill Coghill: with a permanent set and apron stage. Hamlet, Peter Glenville.

Richard II: 1936: produced by John Gielgud. Richard II, David King Wood.

(*Photographs by Cyril Arapoff*).

Winter's Tale: 1946: produced by Nevill Coghill, in the gardens of Exeter College.

(*Photograph by Kenneth Parker*).

112. SHAKESPEARE IN THE UNIVERSITIES: CAMBRIDGE: productions of the Marlowe Dramatic Society:

1. *Troilus and Cressida*: 1922 (see No. 96).

2. 1929-46:
i-iii, v, vi: *King Lear*: 1929. Lear, Peter Hannen.
iv, ix, x: *King Lear*: 1944.
vii, viii: *King Lear*: 1938.
xi: *Julius Caesar*: 1936.
xii, xiii: *Antony and Cleopatra*: 1934,
xiv, xvi, xvii: *Antony and Cleopatra*: 1946.
xv: *Winter's Tale*: 1945.

(*Photographs by Ramsey and Muspratt, Cambridge: photographs of King Lear 1929, by courtesy of Hills and Saunders Cambridge*).

3. 1932-43:
i-viii: *Hamlet*: 1932.
ix-xi: *The Tempest*: 1938.
xii-xiv: *Othello*: 1943.

(*Photographs by Ramsey and Muspratt, Cambridge: the small photographs of Hamlet by courtesy of Hills and Saunders, Cambridge*).

All plays shown on these two panels produced by George Rylands.

Since its first Shakespearean production, *Richard II*, in 1910, the Marlowe Society has presented twelve of the plays in nineteen productions. The Society works with its own non-professional producers and designers. Until 1930 all the parts were taken by men: women's parts are now played by women undergraduates.

The only play illustrated here which has an all-male cast is *King Lear*, 1929.

113. ANTONY AND CLEOPATRA: Dec. 1946: Piccadilly:.directed by Glen Byam Shaw: costumes and settings by Motley: music by Anthony Hopkins.

Cleopatra, Edith Evans; Antony, Godfrey Tearle; Enobarbus, Anthony Quayle; Lepidus, George Howe; Octavius Cæsar, Michael Goodliffe; Thyreus, James Cairncross; Agrippa, Mark Dignam; Proculeius, Richard Warner; Charmian, Nancy Nevinson; Iras, Katherine Blake.

(*Photographs by Houston Rogers: presented by Tennent Plays Ltd.*).

The set was a non-representational permanent structure, which did not aim at reproducing any particular architectural style but at providing the essential elements of the Elizabethan stage—namely, main stage, inner stage or recess, and upper stage or balcony. The inner stage could be shut off, either by a shutter or curtains, to indicate the movement of the action from Egypt to Rome. As in the Elizabethan theatre, the recess could be set so as to give indications of particular localities; as, for example, with a barred door for the monument. In essence a permanent set, it had much of the scenic adaptability of a semi-permanent set; and with the aid of a few scenes played in front of traverse curtains situated just behind the act drop, it enabled the action of the rapidly changing scenes to be perfectly continuous, thereby clarifying it and emphasizing its shape and momentum.

The costumes represented a free treatment of the Renaissance style, with some suggestions of Roman and Egyptian, and were so designed in order to bear the same kind of relationship to early 17th-century theatrical practice as the setting bore to the Shakespearean stage.

114. OLD VIC PRODUCTIONS AT THE NEW THEATRE:

King Lear: 24 Sept., 1946: produced by Laurence Olivier: scenes and costumes designed by Roger Furse.

Lear, Laurence Olivier; Kent, Nicholas Hannen; Gloucester, George Relph; Albany, Cecil Winter; Cornwall, Harry Andrews; The Fool, Alec Guinness; Edgar, Michael Warre; Edmund, Peter Copley; Goneril, Pamela Brown; Regan, Margaret Leighton; Cordelia, Joyce Redman.

(*Photographs by John Vickers*).

115. HENRY V: TWO CITIES—LAURENCE OLIVIER TECHNICOLOUR FILM: 1944: produced and directed by Laurence Olivier, at Denham Studios. (*Stills presented by Two Cities*).

1, 2. Laurence Olivier in the title rôle; Renee Asherson as Princess Katharine; Alice, Ivy St. Helier.
3. *l. to r.* (i) Alice and Princess Katharine. (ii) Duke of Burgundy, Valentine Dyall. (iii) The Dauphin. and the French Dukes on the eve of Agincourt. (iv) King of France, Harcourt Williams, with the Dauphin. (v and vi) Welsh bow-men at Agincourt. (vii) Renée Asherson as Princess Katharine.
4. *l. to r.* (i) Orleans, Francis Lister; the Constable of France and the Dauphin. (ii) Mountjoy, the Herald of France, Ralph Truman. (iii) The Dauphin, Max Adrian. (iv) The Constable, Leo Genn. (v) Fluellen, Esmond Knight; Gower, John Laurie. (vi) French horsemen under fire from the English archers at Agincourt. (vii) Archbishop of Canterbury, Felix Aylmer.

116. SHAKESPEARE IN THE OPEN AIR: Regent's Park Open Air Theatre. THE TEMPEST: 1933: produced by Robert Atkins. Prospero, John Drinkwater; Juno, Marie Burke; Caliban, Robert Atkins.
ROMEO AND JULIET: 1934: produced by Robert Atkins. Juliet, Margaretta Scott; Romeo, Griffiths Jones; Mercutio, Leslie French.
MUCH ADO ABOUT NOTHING: 1939: produced by Robert Atkins. Beatrice, Cathleen Nesbett; Benedick, D. A. Clarke Smith.
PERICLES: 1939: (artificial lighting): produced by Robert Atkins. Marina, Margaret Vines; Pericles, Robert Eddison; Pander, Peter Bennett; Helicammus, W. E. Holloway; Thaisa, Sylvia Coleridge.

117. SHAKESPEARE IN TELEVISION. HAMLET, with John Byron. ROMEO AND JULIET. THE MERCHANT OF VENICE.

MACBETH — 1709 - 1946

I. SPRANGER BARRY (1719-77) AS MACBETH: from the drawing by J. Gwinn, printed by Robert Sayer: mezzotint: *n.d.* Barry was Garrick's chief rival, famous for the 'silver tones' of his lovely voice and for his fine presence and bearing. The artist has depicted the 'entry after the murder' in the traditional manner—in which, presumably, Barry played it—a dagger in each hand, and glancing back over his shoulder to the door of Duncan's chamber. The more natural level of the hands and arms in Garrick (No. II*l.*) is noticeable: c.f. Betterton's advice on gesture: 'in lifting up the hands, to preserve the grace you ought not to lift them above the eyes'.

II. (*r.*) FRONTISPIECE TO MACBETH, ROWE'S SHAKESPEARE: 1709.
Note: the cauldron sinking, as if on a stage trap: Macbeth in contemporary military costume: and the resemblance of the cavern to the design for the Pit of Acheron in Charles Kean's production (No. VI, vii).

(*l.*) GARRICK AS MACBETH: (Bell, 1775): by T. Parkinson, *ad vivam*, engraved Charles White. Compare the costume with that of No. III, and for the curious wig-effect see Catalogue note to No. 48. Does it suggest that we may take seriously the account given by Frederick Reynolds (*op. cit.*) of Garrick's mechanical wig? Reynolds saw Garrick's last performance of *Hamlet*, and had his hair cut that morning by Garrick's wig-maker, one Perkins, who told him 'that when I saw Garrick first behold the Ghost I should see each individual hair of his head stand upright', hoping 'I would reserve a mite of approbation for him, as the artist of this most ingenious mechanical wig'. Reynolds admits he does not know whether this was a hoax or a puff but records that he did *not* see Garrick's hair 'rise perpendicular'. Whatever the truth, there appears to be something more than ordinary theatrical 'distraction' to account for Garrick's appearance in this particular print.

III. GARRICK AND MRS PRITCHARD IN MACBETH: engraved by Valentine Green, after the painting by Zoffany, now in the possession of the Gaekwar of Baroda: 1776: mezzotint. Zoffany painted two versions of this picture, one for Garrick and the other for Mrs Pritchard. In the other, now in the possession of the Garrick Club (No. 386), Macbeth wears a bluish-green coat with scarlet facings and gold lace, scarlet waistcoat and breeches, and white stockings: Lady Macbeth, instead of the black satin dress, wears a dove-grey satin with gold fringe and ermine border.

Mrs Pritchard took her farewell of the stage in this part, with Garrick, in 1768. Theatre legend has it that she knew nothing of the play beyond her own part. Lord Harcourt, who had seen both her and Mrs Siddons, said: 'To say that Mrs Siddons, in one word, is superior to Mrs Pritchard in Lady Macbeth, would be talking nonsense, because I don't think that it is possible . . . she wants the dignity, and above all, the unequalled compass and melody of Mrs Pritchard'. (Doran: *Annals*).

IV. MRS SIDDONS AS LADY MACBETH: painted by G. Harlow, engraved by Robert Cooper: 1822: stipple and line.

In the famous sleep-walking scene where she so boldly defied the Pritchard tradition and put down the candle. Bell's account is: 'She advances rapidly to the table, sets down the light and rubs her hand, making the action of lifting up water in one hand at intervals'. When the management got wind of her intention Sheridan protested, and warned her that 'it would be thought a presumptious innovation'. Mrs Siddons made it the new tradition.

V. MACREADY'S MACBETH:
1. Playbill.
2. MACREADY AS MACBETH: painted by H. Tracey, engraved by T. Sherratt: *n.d.* line and stipple.

3. Drawings of Macready's Covent Garden production of *Macbeth* in 1837: from Scharf's *Recollections* (see No. 73).

VI. CHARLES KEAN AS MACBETH: from the portrait by A. E. Chalon: drawn on stone by R. J. Lane: coloured: proof: 1 Oct., 1840.

In London he played *Macbeth* for the first time at the Haymarket, 6 July, 1840. It was considered 'one of his ablest delineations'. On this occasion Mrs Warner played his Lady Macbeth.

VII. CHARLES KEAN'S MACBETH at the PRINCESS'S: 14 Feb., 1853.
1. Playbill (three sheets), with full historical and antiquarian notes.
2. Nine designs, from the original water-colour sketches in the Victoria and Albert Museum.
(i) Dunsinane (by F. Lloyds); (ii) Dunsinane: interior (Lloyds); (iii) A Glen near Forres (by H. Cuthbert); (iv) The Alarm, after the discovery of the murder of Duncan (by W. Gordon); (vi) The Banquet Scene (by Days): (vii) The Pit of Acheron (the witches' cavern) (by Gordon); (viii) The Witches' Gathering (by T. Grieve); (ix) The Death of Macbeth (by Days & Cuthbert); (x) Iona by Moonlight (by Cuthbert).

(v) Mr and Mrs Charles Kean (Ellen Tree) as Macbeth and Lady Macbeth: (*from a photograph in the Enthoven Collection, Victoria and Albert Museum*). 'No matter what the character that Mrs Kean was assuming, she always used to wear her hair drawn flat over her forehead and twisted tight round her ears in a kind of circular sweep . . . And then the amount of petticoats she wore!' (Ellen Terry: *Story of my Life*).

There are some interesting notes on this production in *Notes and Queries* (7 Ser. VIII, 13 July, 1889) by Cuthbert Bede:

'The witch scene . . . was treated with fog and mist, which, partially clearing away, dimly revealed the three witches, whose vanishing was upwards . . . Gauze curtains were used in all the witch scenes. The bleeding soldier was introduced on a rude litter'.

Of the Banquet Scene he records: 'Much of the business of the scene was done by the Keans between these pillars [of the semi-circular arch] and the foot-lights. The only lights for the banquet were torches stuck in the pillars. . . Kean took his seat on a bench by the front table, so that he and the First Murderer were able to converse apart. When Banquo's ghost was first seen it appeared on the double seat of state by the side of Lady Macbeth. The head of Banquo was illuminated by a strong pale blue light'. Kean remained down-stage after the first disappearance of the ghost, and Lady Macbeth came down to him. Wine was brought 'Turning round to pledge the guests, the L. pillar close to him suddenly became illuminated, Banquo's ghost being seen within it'. In the sleep-walking scene, 'when Mrs Kean entered with the taper she at once placed the taper on a table' At the end of the play, 'in the place of *Exeunt fighting* Macbeth was killed upon the stage, and the tragedy was there ended, the soldiers saluting Malcolm, 'Hail, King of Scotland, hail!' as the curtain fell. I saw Macready in *Macbeth*, and he ended the play in the same way, but Phelps kept to the strict text, and made Macduff bring on Macbeth's head on a pole'.

VIII. SAMUEL PHELPS (1804-78) and MCKEAN BUCHANAN (1823-72) as MACBETH: ISABELLA GLYN AS LADY MACBETH: plates to Tallis (see Nos. 65-72).

IX. HENRY IRVING AS MACBETH: 1875. Drawing by V. W. Bromley. *Illustrated London News*, 15/12/75.

X. IRVING'S MACBETH: 29 Dec., 1888: Lyceum. Souvenir. Drawings by Bernard Partridge and Charles Cattermole.

No. 14 corresponds very closely to the original Hawes Craven design in the Victoria and Albert Museum. Nos. 5 and 9 can be compared with the two photographs of the Sargent paintings of Ellen Terry as Lady Macbeth (National Portrait Gallery and Tate Gallery). Scenes by Hawes Craven, C. and J. Harker, W. Hann, W. Perkins, R. Cane and T. W. Hall.

'*What they said at the time*', *The Graphic* (5/1/89): 'In scenic art England may now be fairly said to stand pre-eminent. With the exception of the Meiningers, who now and then, when at home, are worthy rivals, there is nothing to be seen on continental stages which will compare for *mise-en-scène* with the Lyceum productions'.

Illustrated London News: 'Doré himself might have designed the supernatural portion of the play . . . The conclusion of one act, when the spirits fly in the air and people the wind at the approach of day, is as impressive a picture as the "Brocken" scene in *Faust*, and is literally a triumph of scenic effect'. For this scene (Act IV) Sullivan wrote the music, and the *St James's Gazette* (31/12/88) says: 'When the scene changes from the witches' cave to the shores of a Scotch loch, under a wild stormy sky, the crowd of Hecate's attendant spirits break forth into a magnificent Mendelssohnian chorus'.

The Star (31/12/88), describing the courtyard: 'On the right a cloistered passage, a steep flight of stone steps leading to a gallery, and on the left a huge shaft, at the base of which winds the ascent to the King's chamber. The wind whistles and howls, and the thunder rolls'. Like everyone else, however, *The Star* disapproved of the handling of the ghost scenes, because 'on each appearance of the spectre the stage is suddenly plunged in darkness'.

XI. FORBES-ROBERTSON'S MACBETH: 17 Sept., 1898: Lyceum: with Mrs Patrick Campbell as Lady Macbeth and Robert Taber as Macduff. Taber's performance was outstanding: *The Times* thought Mrs Patrick Campbell's 'wooden', and preferred her in modern plays. Forbes-Robertson's personal make-up was described as 'a living picture of the rude northern soldier—ruddy, robust, unkempt, strong in physical courage, but morally weak'.

XII. BEERBOHM TREE'S MACBETH: 5 Sept., 1911: His Majesty's. Scenes by McCleery, Hawes Craven and J. Harker: costumes designed by Percy Anderson.
I. (i) The Witches' Flight, by McCleery.
(ii) A Barren Heath, by McCleery.
(iii) Corridor in the Palace, by Hawes Craven.
(iv) Room in Macbeth's Castle, by Hawes Craven.
(vi) Courtyard of Macbeth's Castle, by J. Harker.
II. (i) Audience Chamber, by J. Harker.
(ii) Banqueting Hall, by J. Harker.
IV. (i & iii) The Battlements, by McCleery.
Macbeth, H. Beerbohm Tree; Duncan, Edward O'Neill; Malcolm, Basil Gill; Donalbain, Ion Swinley; Banquo, J. H. Barnes; Macduff, Arthur Bourchier; Lady Macbeth, Violet Vanbrugh; Gentlewoman, Laura Cowie.
(Daily Mirror photographs).
There are signs of the times in the not-very-kind notice of The Times. It was, after all, only twelve months before 'Barkerised Shakespeare' was to shock, astonish and delight the London playgoer. Discontent with realistic spectacle was in the air. 'Beauty is the thing this revival aims at, first and last. There is nothing ugly in the representation—not even the witches . . . The sleep-walking scene was a scene of beauty. Flights of steps zig-zagged precipitously from the base to the very top of the scene. Evidently in an incident of sleep-walking it is appropriate that the sleep-walker should really have some walking to do. Lady Macbeth went slowly up and up, always beautifully. There was beauty again in the banqueting scene, barbaric beauty (including a fierce dance of retainers), and even the ghost of Banquo was a beautiful ghost . . . Of course, we were never shaken with terror. Terror (on the stage) has had its day'. (Times: 6/9/11).

An advance notice of the death warrant presently to be served upon the Kean-Irving-Tree tradition of spectacular Shakespeare!

XIII. HENRY AINLEY AND SYBIL THORNDIKE IN MACBETH: 24 Dec., 1926: Prince's: produced by Lewis Casson: scenes and costumes designed by Charles Ricketts.
The Witches, Zillah Carter, Ivan Berlyn, Ronald Kerr; the Sergeant, Hubert Carter; Banquo, Lewis Casson; Macduff, Basil Gill.
(Photographs by Bertram Park).

XIV. (r.) MACBETH AT THE OLD VIC.
(1) John Gielgud as Macbeth (17 March, 1930).
(Photograph by Pollard Crowther).
'Every good performance of any Shakespeare play is recognisable by the fact that it arouses fresh shock at something which one knows so well that one takes it for granted—to each spectator his own shock, of course . . . My own occurred when Macbeth came away from the murder carrying with incredible clumsiness both daggers as witnesses. To experience this shock is to believe in the murder, and this again is to believe in the actor'. (James Agate: 19 March, 1930).
(2) Macbeth: 12 Nov., 1932: produced by Edward Carrick (son of Gordon Craig) and Harcourt Williams: scenes and costumes designed by Edward Carrick.
Macbeth, Malcolm Keen: Lady Macbeth, Margaret Webster.
(3) Macbeth: 26 Nov., 1937: produced by Michel St. Denis: scenes and costumes designed by Motley.
Macbeth, Laurence Olivier; Lady Macbeth, Judith Anderson; Macduff, Ellis Irving.
(Photographs by J. W. Debenham).

(l). JOHN GIELGUD'S MACBETH: 8 July, 1942: Piccadilly: produced by John Gielgud: décor by Michael Ayrton and John Minton: costumes by Michael Ayrton.
Macbeth, John Gielgud; Lady Macbeth, Gwen Ffrangcon Davies; Duncan (and Seyton) Nicholas Hannen; Messenger, Alan Badel; the Doctor, A. Bromley Davenport; Banquo, Leon Quartermaine.
(Photographs by Gordon Anthony).

XV. MACBETH—THREE EXPERIMENTS:
(1) At the Playhouse, Liverpool: 2 May, 1934: produced by William Armstrong.

(2) In modern dress: Sir Barry Jackson's production, directed by H. K. Ayliff: 6 Feb., 1928: Court.
Macbeth, Eric Maturin; Lady Macbeth, Mary Merrall; Malcolm, Laurence Olivier; Macduff, Scott Sunderland: Banquo, Marshall Sheppard; the Witches, Muriel Aked, Una O'Connor, Joan Pereira.
(*Photographs by Lenare: reproduced by permission from copies in the Enthoven Collection*).

(3) Produced by George Rylands, for the Marlowe Society, Cambridge, 1939: in the costume of 'The '45' or Bonnie Prince Charlie: scenes designed by Michael Majendie.
(*Photographs by Ramsey and Muspratt*).

XVI. MACBETH: as played by an undergraduate for the O.U.D.S.
(*Photograph: Cyril Arapoff*).
Compare the 'traditional' make-up: Charles Kean: Phelps: Buchanan: Irving: Gielgud.

XVII. MACBETH AT STRATFORD: 1946: produced by Michael MacOwan: costumes and settings by Frederick Crooke.

Macbeth, Robert Harris; Lady Macbeth, Valerie Taylor.
(*Photographs: Angus McBean*).

The producer's aim was to set the play firmly in the period to which it belongs—the Jacobean. The permanent set was intended to suggest that the play was being performed in the hall of a great house. It provided equivalents of the Shakespearean main, inner and upper stages, thus securing complete continuity for the action and enabling the characters to move without any break from one scene to another in different parts of the set, each area being lighted when it was brought into use. For scenes between Macbeth and his wife, the recess was used as a small room to give greater intimacy and reality. Painted cloths and set pieces were used behind the permanent structure of staircases and bridge for the larger scenes.